ROGER ELWOOD

BOOK TWO IN THE *ANGELWALK* SAGA

A
NOVEL

WORD PUBLISHING
Dallas · London · Vancouver · Melbourne

Library of Congress Cataloging-in-Publication Data

Elwood, Roger
    Fallen angel : a novel / by Roger Elwood.
        p.   cm.
    ISBN 0-8499-3239-4
    I. Title.
    PS3555.L85F35   1991
    813'.54—dc20   90-23594
                                                                  CIP

Printed in the United States of America

2 3 4 5 6 7 8 9 LBM 7 6 5

John Long
—for being the guy who brought us together

Joey Paul
—for being an editor who inspires

And those other
brothers and sisters in Christ
for whom the Great Commission
is not simply money earned
in the work they do

Foolish [mortals and demons] imagine that because judgment for evil is delayed, there is no justice, but only accident here below. [But it] is sure as life, it is sure as death!
—*Thomas Carlyle*

Acknowledgments

A VERY SPECIAL THANKS TO JOEY PAUL; WHEN people told me that this man was considerate, intelligent, honest, and a strong believer in Jesus Christ, well, they were hitting the mark precisely.

Then there is Debbie Hannas, Joey's associate, and a remarkably well-organized and wonderful asset to everyone fortunate enough to work with her.

And some other terrific individuals at Word: Laura Kendall who spearheaded the acquisition of the audio rights of the first *Angelwalk* book as well as with this second one; Laura Minchew whose view of quality juvenile publishing is encouraging indeed; Carol Bartley who sees the need for superior reference works for young people; plus Nancy Norris, Patti Daigle and Judy Gill who have been exceedingly helpful to me.

Let me also mention several more: Tom Williams, a transcendantly talented and creative art director who views writers with respect, and whose own talent borders on genius; Charles "Kip" Jordon and Byron Williamson, two heavyweight executives who remain very nice human beings; Jim Nelson Black who provided initial and much-needed support; Noel Halsey, whose own excitement is more than a little appreciated; Lee Gessner, who has been encouraging indeed; Rob Birkhead, a brilliant craftsman; Dave Moberg, who was there early on; and Ernie Owen, to whom I owe a great deal.

And I must voice a sincere debt of gratitude to Sheri Livingston Neely in the final stages of editing the manuscript.

Nor can I forget Jan Dennis without whose help there would never have been *any* book entitled *Angelwalk*, let alone a sequel!

I'll conclude by thanking more than a hundred thousand *Angelwalk* readers; their enthusiasm enabled the publication of *Fallen Angel*.

Foreword

I HAVE TO SAY THAT *FALLEN ANGEL*, A SEQUEL TO *Angelwalk*, is a far superior masterwork. It may be quite unnerving to many readers, and it will certainly prod the consciences of countless numbers of them.

In my own book, *Battle for the Bible*, I named some of the evangelical leaders who seemed to be presiding over the declining numbers of those who hold to the inerrancy of Scripture. In *Fallen Angel*, Roger Elwood does not give us names but goes one step further, by probing the satanic mindset behind the accelerating campaign to tear the Body of Christ away from that most precious and necessary of moorings, the Holy Scriptures, God's Word given to mankind.

You may not agree with every word presented in this gripping work of fiction, but you will be fascinated by an authentic scripturally-sound and rather explosive presentation of Satan as seen through the eyes of his pathetic follower, Observer, for whom we feel the utmost sympathy and whose tragedy is also that of any human being who turns his back on the Living Christ.

There is little doubt that reading *Fallen Angel* could prove to be a greater life-changing experience than would be the case with any other Christian novel in recent memory—and that it will be much discussed over the coming months as Christians everywhere ponder the different characterizations in the book, and wonder how many, if any, are far from being entirely fictitious. I can say one thing: Elwood's uncompromising grasp of the reality of the merchandizing, publishing and commercial side of the evangelical community has in it enough accurate data and clear-eyed truth to warrant those involved taking a hard look at themselves, and starting immediately to correct the imbalances.

DR. HAROLD LINDSELL

Introduction

"YOUR BOOK CHANGED MY LIFE!" THE MIDDLE-aged woman said as I signed for her a copy of *Angelwalk*. "It alerted me once and for all to the reality of Satan."

I thanked her, and she left — but her words stayed with me.

"Your book changed my life."

Could a writer be greeted with anything finer than that, as simple and yet as profound as that acknowledgment was? Favorable reviews are pleasant and indeed reassuring. Strong sales help perpetuate the ministry of writing. But it isn't until words get beyond the paper on which they are printed and enter a reader's life and have *impact* that the very point of writing, its reason for being, is achieved.

For the Christian who is a writer, all of this is doubly important. The knowledge that what he does can be used by the Lord to enrich the lives of each book's readers, well, I submit the thesis that for the Christian as writer, there *must* be *no* other primary motivation. If his career is *just* to make money, to gain fame, then the Lord may honor the writing anyway because He can always work with the most imperfect of vessels whenever He so chooses. But—and this is a big one—how much better, how much more ennobling if we give back to Him our very best motivations rather than the crumbs from some egocentric desire.

Why go ahead and do another book in what we might call the *Angelwalk* vein?

Because such a story told only from the unfallen angelic viewpoint is not complete. It is one third of the way, but not more than that. So that is why I wrote *Fallen Angel*. I thought it would be potentially edifying if we were able to learn more about the *why* of Satan's fall from Heaven, along with some glimpses of the *how*, that is, how he intends to try to accomplish victory in the spiritual warfare of which he is chief instigator and, ultimately, doomed combatant.

This seemed to be more clearly achievable if told from essentially the demonic point of view, which allows for insights not otherwise possible. It is crucial in any warfare, but especially that which is spiritual, to understand your enemy, and to make sure that you have sufficient armament to defend yourself.

I also feel that Observer represents some of the most frustrating traits of human nature. There are indeed many, many Christians who simply observe the evil around them, moan and groan over the state of the world, and proclaim, "The Lord's in charge. He'll handle everything." What they are saying, in effect, is that they *need not* do anything. In the case of Observer, a fallen angel, the opposite is true. He looks around, sees Satan's power, and assumes that he *cannot* do anything.

As we know, there are people very much akin to Observer, deeply involved in habitual, addictive sin, beguiled by Satan to such an extent that they say either, "I can get out anytime I want," or, like Observer, "I can't break away no matter how hard I try," and believe every awful, corrosive, fatal word.

How much truth has Observer stumbled upon over the many centuries of his existence? How many falsehoods remain in the corridors of his befouled intellect? And which is which? Does he truly know? Remember, Satan, the master of all those like Observer, is also the Arch Deceiver. Since he is able to deceive human beings, from Adam and Eve onward, would it be at all difficult for him to pull the shroud of deception over pitiable Observer?

These are questions with which readers will need to deal for themselves. They will have to confront each and every word of his story, to discern where divine truth breaks through, and where demonic entrapment runs rampant.

Please note that to fully show the mindset of Satan and his demons, certain words have been used that are quite strong. No Christians speak these words found in the book you are reading—only demonic entities or human beings held in their sway. Sometimes the language we hear from the people around us denotes what they are really like, whom they really serve. So it is, occasionally, within these pages. Please be prepared.

Fallen Angel now begins, entirely from his perspective, this demonic journalist who spins his tale from the Casting Out until that final of all days, when any thought of possible independence, any hope of breaking the chains, will end as he and his brethren continue to play the perverse and awful game of following their leader . . . into the lake of fire forever and ever.

ROGER ELWOOD

A Book of
the Days
of Observer

Once an Angel
of Light

*In the tinkling laughter of a particular moment amid the journey of that special hour if time were any longer time, there is found beside that path of legend called Angelwalk what surely must have been a treasured book of the ancient past, pages nearly gone, lying near a kindly lion's paws at temporary rest. Only some meaningless old scraps remain, none displaying anything legible except the last fragile bits of a few lost words . . . A Bo.k of the Da.s of Obse..ver, Once an Ang— ***

Prologue

I STAND BEFORE THE SCARLET FLAMES. OTHERS OF my kind already have been forced over the edge into this massive lake of fire and brimstone.

(Where are you now, Sunday and Moody and Calvin? Laughing at us from your righteousness? Millions used to scorn your stern messages, crying, in their rebuke, "More love! More love! More love!" and, in the process, sending countless multitudes to hell, that road of infamous damnation greased with the deceptions of an emasculated gospel.)

The cries of my comrades fill the air.

From sitting at the feet of the Almighty to being crushed underfoot!

The end at which they scoffed, and seduced others into doing similarly, that end we relegated to the annals of mere religious myth, now enveloping us for all of eternity.

The dreams we shared!

What plans we had to re-enter Heaven with conquering hordes who would take over and establish a new order.

On the throne of the once-Almighty he was. The hosts of Heaven cowering at his feet. The once golden streets littered with the debris of his victory. There was pain now, tears, the pathetic agonies of defeated angels, the dread of redeemed ones from all of history. Satan the victor! His own obscene fantasies now the reality of eternity.

Gone.

Now ashes. Now so pointless . . . diseased imaginings, mocking memories that would accuse us, accuse us all forever.

Forever. . . .

How fair can that be?

(A familiar argument that, the cliché of cynical minds.)

Such a thought is only fleeting, buried by the ravaging images of many centuries, images that project the true truth.

How many times have I stood on the sidelines, watching, often sickened by what I saw, and yet offering no protest?

How many victims from Auschwitz and Dachau and Treblinka have fallen at my feet, and looked up and saw me as they died, asking, "Please, please, do something! Stop the slaughter. For the love of God, do something!"

But I cannot. I cannot. I cannot.

Because I belong to those causing the infamy.

Countless blind humans have asked the same question: If God is just, and loving, and forgiving, how could He *ever* have allowed the existence of Hell?

But I know the answer, truly I do, know the answer in the sight of those gassed or cremated Jews, men, women, and children condemned by captors who were our puppets.

Yet these, as tragic as they are, do not hold the answer in its entirety. Others as well, such as the boys slaughtered by a madman who tormented them unto death, and then made love to their cold, abused bodies and, finally, buried them, thinking they would never be missed or discovered, and that he could go on and on, finding pleasure in abominable ways of darkness.

That question again, yes, yes: *How fair is it for God to condemn anyone to pain without end?*

There is a wretched smile on my face now, a smile without joy, a smile dripping with irony, a smile as I think of those fools so blind to so obvious an answer.

It *is* everywhere, you know, on the front page of every newspaper, on the screen of every television set, everywhere indeed, each time terrorists explode their bombs, each time gangs engage in drive-by killings, each time—

How fair if there were *not* the punishment of Hell for the damned, mandated by countless accusing legions of victims?

Oh, God, I scream silently in my mind, my tormented mind, *oh, God, I know the truth about us, and the unmitigated justice of what You are forcing upon us, their dead, dead bodies like a perverse path on which I step as it leads to the flames.*

I cannot bear the panoply any longer. At the beginning, there was only Cain. And now so *many!*

I turn.

Beside me is Lucifer, his face festering.

"The book?" he asks.

I point to the bits and pieces of my journal on the ground.

It is open to a certain page. Satan glances at this. If he could cry, he would, the tears flowing, but he cannot. There is little emotion left and even now no repentance.

"Leave it behind," he tells me. "Leave it for the useless thing that it is, all it has ever been."

I nod.

Indeed, once mighty arch-angel, Son of the Morning.

But what is the use? There is no one left to heed. . . .

"It does not matter anymore, Observer," he says, my expression making the reading of thoughts unnecessary.

He is unsmiling.

"All those prophecies," he says. "We made our victims scoff, we deceived so expertly, cutting into harmless little pieces the great tapestries of divine truth. The tragedy of it is that we became entrapped in our own lies by refusing to heed the same truths."

But not only demons, I say to myself with words he cannot hear because they are unspoken. *Look at so many of the television evangelists who speak of men becoming gods. That is a lie, but they wrap it so tightly around themselves that they and it become as one, and there is no longer any way to separate the two. And so they must go on repeating the deception until it claims their destiny, a destiny they foist upon many of those who look up at them as purveyors of truth.*

Satan turns but briefly, says something I don't quite understand, and then jumps into the flames.

I look in the same direction.

Darien! The voyager treading the path called Angelwalk, facing his doubts, and eliminating these one by one until that glorious moment when all the heavenly hosts welcomed him back into Heaven.

"I could not," I shout to him. "I tried but I could not. His hold was too strong, too—"

I remember so vividly one passage from Darien's journal: *Lucifer.*

Gathered around him are a thousand of his demons... they become one, their forms blending, and at the same time the real Satanic self returns but bigger, even more revolting, red sores erupting... his breath the stuff of cesspools. He raises a hand, commanding Observer, who goes, whimpering, standing before Lucifer, becoming a part of the ungodly union. *

"You were right, Darien of Angelwalk," I add in my final words to him. "Your book told the truth."

... the final moment of judgment on all the fallen angels — Mifult, D'Seaver, D'Filer, Observer, each and every on the rim of the lake of fire, and then over the edge. Finally Lucifer himself.... The defiance is gone. But not the results of countless centuries of deviltry. His countenance is even worse—however, instead of the flaunting of his powers, the perverse pride in what he has caused, there is only terror as he hears the cries of his fellow angels like a thick fog swirling around him. *

My book, my book....

A chronicle of all that I am, all that I have seen, all that was wasted, all that could have been but never, never, never was.

It will not be completed now, a fragmented work dropped by the wayside perhaps, and trampled underfoot, eventually becoming just forgotten dust, this pitiable attempt at an overall record of Satan's time on earth, my master's vain and doomed effort at a kind of unholy writ into which all the separate bits and pieces written by my hosts over the centuries would be compiled and made available to the fallen elect.

Fallen elect. . . .

Satan's ravings ring loudly in memory, the sight of massed demons screaming their blood-thirsty approval somehow as vivid as though happening at that very instant.

I shake myself out of that recollection as I see that my familiar former comrade is still so near to me.

Darien.

The wandering angel, filled with questions—uncertain, yes, capricious, perhaps, but not fallen—and finally welcomed back into Heaven to the chorus of angels of light, and the magnificence of the Holy Trinity.

Oh, Darien, where you go soon, along the path called Angelwalk toward Mount Sinai—oh, how I yearn to be by your side.

I wave sadly to dear Darien, my former comrade who wanted nothing but salvation for me. But I was too weak, too—

I step closer to the edge.

The heat touches me!

As everything once more floods back into my consciousness—everything indeed, small and great, no matter how hard I have fought to submerge the recollections, the bits and pieces of the mosaic of all that had gone before—it comes, this tidal wave of infamy, to be repeated over and over as I stand amongst the flames without end.

The faces of my comrades in front of me, their torment so strident as they cry from it — surely I am not like them, surely I do not deserve what they—

Yet surely I do, I know that, Lord, Lord, if only saying Your name *now* could change my destiny—but I cannot hope for such a miracle, I cannot hope at all because *my* lord stands among the flames.

He reaches out that cankered hand as he sees me. His pus-dripping lips move. He beckons. Only now do I resist for an instant fleeting. And then, as ever—

I come, lord. I come.

And surrender to my destiny.

As I enter my punishment, the memories rage as scornful medusas from the flames to assault me, screeching with demented fury at the failed and evil plans Satan had made so carefully, along with his clever human allies, especially those with their plans for a pivotal assassination, all the way up to that climactic time of confrontation, that final, total Armageddon, and along with these fragments from generations past, there was the foretold anguish.

Foretold. . . .

Oh, yes, it was. We knew the prophecies, we knew the prophecies so well. For Satan, in that latter part of the twentieth century, before we were banished to the lake of fire, the years that passed were a period of planning. My master knew the end times were coming always closer, the momentum accelerating. He could not relax for an instant. And he drove the rest of us always further, more and more acts of appalling barbarity.

In those final days, he had managed to get to a group of communist hardliners, not altogether a difficult task given the atheism that formed the basis for everything they were, every thought, every word, every deed. Now they were planning a grand strategy that would bring power back into their hands, and dispose of Reformer.

Then there were the terrorists, the fanatical Muslims for whom any strike against American interests was pure joy to contemplate, whether it be at oil pipelines in friendly Middle Eastern countries, or at army bases elsewhere, or wherever their utter madness drove them.

Soon these craven minions in allegiance to Lucifer would attack a single target in the western part of the United States itself, causing calamitous devastation.

Satan could hardly wait, could hardly wait to stand among the shards, he and the rest of our demonkind, and hungrily pick off many of the rising souls who then would be flung directly into Hell, their screams the elixir of Satan's psycho-erotic fantasies-become-reality.

But the moment had not quite arrived. There was time, in that final period of history, to think back, to remember, to relive. . . .

Part I

*J*esus Christus Theou Huios Soter.
I am sitting on the sand in the Sinai Desert. I have left my
host back in Jerusalem. But I will have to return to that
body later, and feed these thoughts to him in retrospect.
This host is one human being whom Satan and I share.

Jesus Christus Theou Huios Soter.

Jesus Christ, Son of God, Savior.

He stands before me, tired, alone, hungry—the physical
part of Him, of course—and I look up at this wondrous Man,
the sun shining off His magnificent flowing mane.

"You could have been *my* master," I say, my words filled
with a pleading acquired over many years of considering the
consequences of my actions, the actions of others like me.

"Yes, that is true, Observer," Jesus replies.

He knows that I am with Him, though His death will not
come for three years. He knows because He is Who He is, deity
and humanity resident as one.

"You could have stood before Lucifer and rejected him,"
Jesus continues, "but you chose not to do so."

There is in His words a touch of weariness, weariness in that part of Him which is flesh and blood—and, as well, a prophetic knowingness that can come only from the other aspect of Himself, that which is linked directly with Heaven, and always will be so, the humanity ultimately discarded after the future resurrection and beyond that, the glorious ascension back into the Heaven that we all knew as home eons ago.

He sits down next to me on the sand for a moment.

"Many others will choose over the centuries ahead," He adds. "Many will mock, and turn away, as you did, Observer."

"Oh, I did not mock You," I protest anxiously. "I—"

"Is rejection anything else, Observer?" He interrupts not unkindly, a patient tone obvious.

I want to protest, but the One who is never wrong is right once again.

"Do you *know* what lies ahead?" He asks.

I want to say that I do not, that I have read or heard nothing except what Satan allows, but it would not be truthful if I did that. I have glimpsed on scrolls of papyrus the words of the old prophecies, and they do offer such strong harbingers. But though I serve the Arch Deceiver, the master of lies, how can I stoop to his devices before the Source of all truth? (Such denials would be as ice, quickly melting under the heat of the desert sun.)

"Yes . . . " I reply, all-feeling save the deepest sorrow bled from me by anticipation of the realities to follow.

"The Deceiver deceives himself, and all who have followed," Jesus remarks.

"He tries," I say, "truly he tries. So many of us have been about to break away for a very long time. Perhaps, before it is too late, we will do so someday."

Jesus looks at me, not with contempt but pity.

"The drunkard thinks he can break the shackles of his debauchery, but falls in a stupor before the wine press," He tells me and then drifts into silence.

I, too, have nothing to say for several moments.

Satan has not as yet tempted the Son of Man. That is to come. I have snuck away, to be with Him. Before, I was with Him at the River Jordan, and I saw the Holy Spirit descend in the form of a dove, and God announce the blessed reality of the Savior.

Jesus knew I was there. But it was not only me of whom He was aware. Satan as well. And thousands of fellow demons shrieking.

Shrieking. . . .

Oh, how that sound, heard many times before over the awful years, how it chilled me.

As the flood waters arose, as Noah and his family and the animals were locked in that clumsy old ark, as people beat on the huge wooden door, screaming for refuge, even as they were swept away by the instrument of God's judgment, water which they needed to live, now their executioner—it became clear that Satan had lost this battle.

While being so near to victory, or thus it seemed, he saw the corruption he midwifed spread throughout the inhabited part of the world, men engaging in evil pursuits to an extent unknown until then. Yet those seduced by him finally drowned in a kind of baptism—and wasn't that it, really, the baptism of the wicked. But instead for them it wasn't a ceremony of cleansing—for the world as a physical entity, yes, but not for the students who so eagerly followed their demonic teacher. For them it was a baptism unto damnation. Water that later in the Jordan would touch the body of God Incarnate and proclaim divinity, now sweeping them away, but Satan remaining, to take up again with those who would come later.

Shrieking. . . .

As animals the demons cried, wounded beasts.

And then at Sodom and Gomorrah, when the fire of judgment rained down on those places of depravity.

Shrieking. . . .

First water and then fire and brimstone.

Always the same. God striking back in righteous anger. Satan retreating for a time.

And now—

Another defeat. The most pivotal of all. Not in a moment of spectacular inter-galactic violence, with laser-like swords flying, the wrath of Holiness.

So quiet it was in the human realm, there at the the Jordan, unseen by nearly all the world's population at the time.

Multitudes spoke not at all. They stood transfixed by the dove. No one uttered a single word.

But not so in the demonic netherworld, not quiet at all. Leathery wings were flapping. Rage was volcanic. If Satan had had the power, he would have leapt upon the body of the carpenter and torn the flesh off, blood running in the Jordan.

Instead he could only shrink back, cower in hatred. And—

Shrieking. . . .

Jesus knew, of course. As He was arising from the water, the dove settling upon Him so briefly, He looked not at Satan, not at Mifult or DuRong, at *none* of them but me, at Observer, reluctant as ever, Observer who had convinced himself that he was *with* the others but not *of* them. Surely now He was saying that I could cross over, that I could shed the bondage—and yet I saw those eyes of His, moist not from the waters of baptism but tears at once human and divine, and He turned away, toward the beckoning cross three years hence, and I was left behind, my own shrieks part of the cacophony, inseparable.

Yes, I know about shrieking, shrieking that I hear now, for I have preceded Satan in the wilderness, and he is coming to join us, angry that I got there first, as always paranoid about who might be betraying him, which is not unlike the kettle calling the pot black.

I step back. I think I hear *Jesus Christus* whisper goodbye, and yet how can I be sure? His voice is soft, of such low pitch as to be hardly audible.

His hand reaches out toward me.

Theou Huios . . . Soter.

Oh, Son of the living God, member of triune divinity, were it to be so, were it to be—

I extend my pitiable talon, so deformed that I am shamed I have nothing better to offer, but He shrinks not. He smiles with such beauty.

Come....

I hear Him. He is actually pleading. He wants me to throw aside—

And then Satan comes between us, in ways infinitely more profound than can ever be expressed through the contrivance of words.

Yet I rebel against my master. I tell him that I have had enough. I reject him forever, and choose another Lord, for Satan is no longer worthy, he has never been worthy, and I tread him underfoot, like dung discarded with disgust, and I reach my Soter, falling before Him as Satan watches, and He welcomes me back into His kingdom ... immediately I am translated before God's throne, and the unfallen ones issue forth with a chorus of sublime welcome.

No.

I have been with Evil far too long. It is not that I cannot, but it *is* that I do not.

I step back.

Snarling with contempt, Satan orders me to return to Jerusalem to guard our host while he, Satan, tarries with Christ.

The hand of *Jesus Christus* is still extended, still mine to touch, to take hold of.

An instant of time.

Not enough. All of eternity would never be enough.

Farewell, Blessed One....

Soon I am back with our host, back with Judas.

It did not begin then, of course, not there in the wilderness, not at the time of the Flood, not even in the Garden. It began for all of us, for Satan, for myself, for our comrades back before there was a planet named Earth, before there were galaxies, before there was life of any kind but ours, walking the streets of Heaven, singing the praises of Almighty God.

And it would end on a field strewn with bodies, a defeat for all our malignant entities.

But in the meantime, between then and now, oh, what I have had to experience. I have been so close to telling the master that I could not take any more of it, so close—

Always I have pulled back, my disgust buried by the enslavening habits of my kind.

Double-minded. Yes. Yes.

Again it returns, persistent, never far from recollection, that accusatory verse of Scripture read a very long time before: "A double-minded man is unstable in all his ways."

"Not only a man," I say outloud.

"What are you babbling about?" asks a fellow demon, his face contorted in agony.

"Nothing," I reply. "Nothing."

That you would understand.

I was there when Jesus cast out the demons from the Gadarene maniac, and certain of my kind went into that herd of swine, and then they all plunged over the cliff's edge to their death. Those fellow demons did not die, of course; they and I are spirit, with immortality. But it was a statement by Christ, a statement that when the Holy Spirit moves in, demons cannot remain even though they are legion.

Oh, how they shrieked and wailed and lamented.

"Another defeat!" weeped one.

"One of the worst!" a second joined him.

"But there are other subjects," the first said, bouncing back from momentary depression.

"The Pharisees, the Saduccees!" the second agreed.

"All except Nicodemus," the first added. "He's too wise, too strong. We should not waste any effort on him. We have the others. That is enough."

I was there when Jesus healed those who were blind, who were deaf, who were lame.

I saw their faces, their joy.

I saw my kind leaving their bodies, running scared.

I was in the tomb with Lazarus.

I saw his spirit return to his body. And his spirit saw me.

"You cannot have me as you thought!" he proclaimed.

"*I* never wanted you," I reminded him.

"Are you so sure?" he asked.

Behind him the terrifying sounds of rampaging demons loosed from a dark, damned domain, trying to thwart this greatest of all the miracles.

"Stop him!" they called in unison. "Stop him, Observer!"

"I cannot!" I screamed back to them, enraged at their deception. As if I could stop the very Son of God!

*T*he death, burial, and resurrection of Christ.

I was once surprised that I gave so much thought to that unforgettable series of epochal events since they were intrinsically contrary to the totality of my existence, of the existence of all those like myself, in subservience as we were to the Prince of Darkness—and yet those occasional, compelling moments of retrospection, sometimes as though possessed of a resolve, a will of their own seem to *force* themselves to the surface of my awareness, while nothing I do can stem their inexorable advance—yet sometimes they are even *allowed* to return (dare I say summoned?) as I grew weary of all the despicable deeds of which I was a part, however oblique that participation may have been, and seek some foolish solace in a personal fantasy to which none of the others has ever been privy, a fantasy in which I learn that that death, that burial, that resurrection were for me as well, that I will not in fact join the despicable damned of the ages, and will be allowed to return to Heaven's glory, washed clean by the same crimson flow—but then reality intrudes, and the fantasy is never more than that . . . yet these moments prove so profound, so unas-sailable in their supreme display of ultimate love, forgiving love, sacrificial love, love that was so much the antithesis of the very *raison d'être* of Satan's existence—which made my fantasy all the more ludicrous, a fact I had had to face if I were to be honest about him and myself and those around me, and all that was portended for the lot of us, acknowledging that indeed our very existence validified the necessity of what the Son of God endured as the only alternative, the only cleansing act that could mitigate what we had wrought in our wake . . . and so I kept returning to these fragments of recollection, like the proverbial moth fascinated by the flickering shades and shapes of the flames before it—for truly it *was* I, Observer, once an angel, once a being who would have celebrated the foretold act of sacrifice and redemption to which I was intimate witness, it was I who was standing in shame before the Cross as I tried to *will* myself into the same cackling howls of perverse delight that my nearby demonic comrades displayed, wallowing in the conviction to which we all clung, the conviction, fragile, desperate, that this was the end of it, the age-old war between God and Satan for the control of the vast expanse of creation, that all those ancient prophecies were but the vain and deluded ravings mostly of old men . . . and though my fellow fallen seemed to have been seduced by such poppycock, yet I failed, failed miserably in my doomed effort to be satiated with temporary joy at the thought of evil transcendent and triumphant—and, thus, I became instead inexpressibly sad, perhaps more so than the mother of Jesus, or the apostle who loved Him most deeply, perhaps more so than any or all of them, as I, too, looked up into that tormented face, seeing the trickles of blood from under the thorny crown, hearing the groans of pain as the body twitched and shook and wrenched in final agony . . . even so, words of exquisite supplication escaped softly and with infinite tenderness past those pale and twisted lips, a supplication not rooted in condemnation, not seeking the damnation of those responsible but rather a supplication begging God to *forgive* the architects of this infamy—and then that final gasp, a small sound really, hardly audible, lasting only for an instant, that final acknowledgment signifying it was finished for Him that it was indeed over ... which all of us, the band of fallen ones who attended that moment, took as utterly incontestable testimony to our victory after so long a time, a victory we celebrated gleefully for three wonderful days of unleashed activity—perhaps frenzy would be more accurate—in which we tormented the eleven remaining apostles with crushing doubt and despair ... relishing this, the pervading ecstasy of it for us, loving every moment of melancholy we midwifed . . . until that Morning, breaking away from the others, when I thought that I alone had visited the Tomb ... I saw, instead, that I was joined by another, hardly unknown to me, clothed in shimmering radiance—as I once had been but now stripped of it—another who told me that my kind had lost after all, that our jubilation was impetuous and ill-fated, that indeed Christ was not there, that He had arisen, that I should go and tell the others that their awful ravings were as doomed as their ultimate destiny, and as I nodded, my very being shuddering at the gravity of what had been said, stirring up images that I, like the other fallen, had tried hard, oh so very hard, to wipe from our consciousnesses ... I then saw Mary Magdalene coming forlornly up the narrow pathway to the Tomb, and I whispered, with assumptive despair, "Good-bye, Darien, good-bye, my once-friend," hurrying finally to the multitudes of demonkind, my funereal words of utter and inescapable damnation portended washing over them like a toxic tidal wave, forcing the entire ignoble horde to our knees in a spasm not of repentant prayer—hardly that, of course—but instead the most pervasive futility we had ever known, rising as it did to envelope us like a strange and encompassing shroud, ironically even at the very moment that our master began to exhort us, demanding in his usual Hitlerian tones that we stand, as his followers, his apostles, holding our heads high, and stop acting with such lamentable cowardice, for we are committed, do not *ever* forget that, we are committed to continuing the struggle against encroaching divinity, and, therefore, we have no choice but to fight on, and on, and yet on still.

*H*e was called Muhammed or Muhammad or Mahomet or however the devil people pronounced it.

Muhammed.

He was my host for many years, from about A.D. 590 until a few years before his death in 632. I generally have not left a host except when the Holy Spirit entered as a result of that host's redemption. With Muhammed it was different. I left, and a demon quite a bit more terrifying slipped in on cloven feet to take over, to drive Muhammed onward with fiercer determination.

But he did write the *Koran* through my guidance. I dictated it virtually word for word—not holy streams of wisdom from the mouth of God, but demonic perversion dressed up to seem noble and profound, a bit silly if it weren't so evil, silly that human beings had the original, and so many of them settled for a counterfeit written by a demon under the remote-control guidance of Lucifer the Magnificent.

I chuckle at that recollection. The *Koran* may well have been my masterpiece. Oh, *The Book of Joseph Smith* was quite good, of course, and so was that tawdry little nonsense which I guided through the hand of Mary Baker Eddy.

But the *Koran!*

Ah, that was the ultimate, truly so, clap-trap religiosity made to seem on a level with God's Word but more like Satan's excrement, droppings from his "bowels" on a stinking dungheap that all of his followers since his death have buzzed around like flies, oblivious to the stench.

And the man himself.

This ludicrous puppet so steeped in his apparent religiosity that he could never realize, not for an instant, that even if the *Koran* were worthy of anything but phlegm from the mouths of any who come in contact with it, if it nevertheless left out the most crucial ingredient of all, it was as nothing, it was as—

Salvation through Jesus Christ and Himself alone.

Not the castrated Allah the Muslims hold so dear. Not the sham religion of Islam that has held tens of millions in its obscene grasp. Not the creepy little men of Libya, Iraq, and Iran, who fight each other as well as their neighbors, and gain near-orgasmic pleasure from tormenting the West, especially the United States, proclaiming their mumbo-jumbo as they turn toward Mecca, those demonic ayatollahs and pathetic Hitlerite dictators and others who are the perfect henchmen of my master, too fanatical, too stupid, too cruel to understand what they *truly* are about, that basically they serve not their countrymen, not the region in which they live, not even the "religion" they profess, but the equally mad ruler of them all.

None of what they profess, none of what they worship, none of what they desire holds any hope for them, for those foolish enough to pay them allegiance.

None of this stinking vomit from hell itself.

Only Jesus the Christ. Only the *real* God made flesh and sacrificed on the cross for the sins of mankind. This same Jesus to whom the rabid and unholy Muslims pay only the most fleeting attention.

I know the right words. I know the right words that could signal my repentance.

I learned them a long, long time ago.

But that is as far as it goes.

And it is not enough.

Not enough at all.

Later, other degenerates guided by Muhammed's lunacy would fit nicely into my master's planning at the advent of the end times, that precipitous moment of infamy in which the Soviets and the Muslims all would be part of the "stew" he concocted. . . .

*I*f Muhammed, then why not a pope or two?

My master has always become delirious with the potential of causing the mighty to tumble from their pedestals.

And what more lofty a pedestal could be there than the one on which each pope has rested since the Roman Catholic Church got away from its moorings in the Early Church and became encrusted with barnacles of hypocrisy that until more recent decades made it more often than not a haven for my kind, and in the case of one of the popes, a host for the writing of my journal?

It is fertile fields for devilry that flourish in the tightest secrecy. Few everyday Catholics have *any* idea what transpires in the inner sanctum of Holy Mother Church. Over the centuries, little more than glimpses have been viewed, and these quite fleeting, a flash or two of life at the Vatican.

That was, from the beginning, a formula for "open sesame" as far as my kind goes. How can so-called holy men be subjected to spirit-testing scrutiny if they are unapproachable, hiding behind ornate walls covered with the art of great painters which give literally a façade of holiness but no way of determining the substance thereof?

Many years later, while seeming extravagant at the time, the escapades of the Bakkers would surely be ranked as infantile infamy when viewed side-by-side with the chicanery flourishing in the midst of priceless treasures of paint, gems, and artifacts—but there is a common thread in such matters, a thread of the lack of the pure light of gospel-directed truth acting as an examining beacon, ferreting out all that dishonors and cheapens the pretended holiness.

Can *I*, a fallen angel, be capable of such thoughts? It is a question oft-repeated during my existence, and the only answer: I have them, therefore I am.

There was more than one bad pope, men who allowed the Roman Catholic Church to become grotesquely fat with materialistic embellishments, to become steeped not in spirituality but onerous superstition. During the medieval period, and particularly the time of the bubonic plague, the Vatican's moral character was as diseased as the bodies of many of its cardinals afflicted by the Black Death, along with countless numbers of those peasants and others foolish enough to continue on as loyal worshipers.

Yes, the bad popes, as they have been called through the centuries, chronicled by human journalists in more than one volume, terrible men doing terrible things to and with a vulnerable Catholicism.

But that one, ah, *that* pope!

A man so evil beneath his outer guise of santification that it could be said that Satan deserved special praise for his cleverness in disguising the monster's true self.

So evil indeed, but also so pervasive that his thinking held the Roman Catholic Church in its grip for a very long time after his death. One man who carries a disease can die in two days, but those he has infected can infect others, and then those others more still until the chain of death goes on for decades.

This pope, this demon-in-fleshly-garb, took over the writing of my journal. He grabbed it out of my control and went on his own way.

I could only stand by and watch. . . .

He wrote of the most extraordinarily blasphemous images. He revelled in erotic perversions of certain biblical precepts. He took *The Song of Solomon* and turned it into a series of masturbatory fantasies from which he received gratification innumerable times.

But no one outside the Vatican knew what he was like. Only the faintest echoes escaped, at once dismissed—ha, ha!—as a satanic attempt to discredit the Holy Father.

Those who served him, those who put him to bed at night and woke him up in the morning, those who put food on his table and bathed him and dressed him, those who were in his presence day after day after relentless day eventually turned sick inside. And when they would protest, he would accuse them of witchcraft or heresy or whatever; if they persisted, the poor fools would be burnt to death or starved until all life was drained from them—or, in some cases, the good-looking ones especially, they would have the honor of sharing his bed, and then be poisoned at the conclusion of their seduction.

The Vatican was hardly a place of virginal intrigue; it had been steeped in byzantine plots and counterplots for centuries. How Peter the Apostle would have reacted if he had witnessed what became of the Early Church, its simple proclamations of redemption massacred by man-made rule after rule, by men grown obese from the labors of those who could barely sustain themselves but nevertheless gave sacrificially to Mother Church.

After the Hideous Pope died, and was entombed, an underling found the journal he had been keeping. On one page were the words:

To Lucifer,
My One and True God

The book, written with quill pen on parchment paper and bound in leather, was turned over to certain members of the Church's hierarchy, who were not totally ignorant of the man's "habits," but they were unprepared for the extent of the depraved nature of his writings. They read every page, horrified by its contents—but rather than destroy it, they took the journal to a secret place in the catacombs under the Basilica, where it would rest, unopened, for centuries.

I know the contents, of course. I looked over his shoulder as he penned the stinking words.

A plan.

A plan for Mother Church.

A plan for the long period of history to follow.

A plan to take whatever good happened to remain, the pure water of the Gospels, and turn it into a cesspool of corruption.

His plan was so brilliant, and it was executed by puppets he left behind, men in whom he had inculcated his Machiavellian designs, some quite willing, others not at all.

This was once the Roman Catholic Church, the personification of the Great Whore of Babylon in that final biblical masterwork, the Book of the Revelation. The Roman Catholic Church did become the evil empire that pope had desired, reeking with foul deeds, draining even further the true faith of the early church fathers, until all that remained was not confined within the corporate structure of the Vatican itself nor any of its satellites throughout the world, but in the worship of the millions of people who still believed in the goodness of Catholicism, even as those earlier ones believed in the goodness of that pope.

But truth cannot be hidden forever. Assisi, Luther, and others caught a glimpse and it inspired them to greatness. God's Word cannot be destroyed and never return, though that is what my master would like to believe, would like *us* to believe.

And yet, in the meantime, nothing could stop the monolith of the Church from spreading the poisonous dogmas with which it infected the Body of Christ. Take purgatory—as long as I have been a demon, I have never seen such a place or state of existence, if you will. There is Heaven; there is Hell. Period. Anything else is a pure concoction to distract from the truth of God's Word, over which my master rejoices.

And Mary!

Ah, yes, virgin Mary, the woman chosen of God to bear the God-man, Christ Jesus.

She lived as an ordinary woman; she died as one. She was honored by being the mother of Jesus, but she is not as Him. Others have elevated her to goddess, even above the Son. And again, my master delighted in such delusion.

As Mary was dying, years after her son was crucified—the beloved apostle John by her side, heeding the Savior's admonition to take care of her since He no longer could—as Mary's spirit was leaving her tired, tired body, she saw me.

"They will be doing awful things, will they not?" she asked, having had a hint, in some moment between her and Almighty God, a hint of what was to come.

"That is so, blessed Mary," I say, pleased more than words could articulate that she did not recoil at my countenance.

"They will be worshiping me," she added.

"Though they will deny this."

"There will be statues of me in every church."

"That is true, dear Mary."

"And your kind will be responsible."

My shoulders slumped, my wings drooped.

"It is as you say, Mary, Mother of God—"

I could not bite off the words in time.

"They will be saying that?" she asked.

I nodded with regret.

"If only they could realize—" she starts to say, then is gone.

On the body of her flesh, growing cold so quickly, are tears that had started to form in her eyes before her heart had ceased its beating, now trickling down her cheeks, just a few actually, and then gone, like mortal life itself.

"Christ has demolished death and our own will, so that we are saved not by our own works, but by His works. . . . Papal power, however, handles us quite differently. Fasting is prescribed, praying, eating butter. If you keep the commands of the pope, then you are saved; if you don't, then you are given over to the devil."

Martin Luther's words were an arrow at the heart of the way Catholicism was being practiced, at the way it was being *controlled* from the rooms and the corridors and even the catacombs of the Vatican.

Satan hated this man, hated the monk's proclamations. He brought about the martyrdom of such Luther loyalists as Henry of Zutphen, that distinguished preacher in Bremen, and ravaged so many others—but he could not in the end destroy Luther himself.

Luther shot the arrows that wounded Catholicism but did not destroy Catholicism. Later, Satan was nothing less than relieved because without this form of worship, Satan's own plans would have been greatly retarded, with one less cloak with which to disguise himself.

On and on the Roman Catholics once marched without hesitation, dispensing error after error, adding needless guilt to the minds and the souls of its heedless subjects, ruling with a medieval mentality even into the Industrial Age.

Until the mid-twentieth century.

Until the pope who took a stand and was poisoned as a result, so soon after he became the Holy Father.

Until the man who succeeded him came to grips with what had been eating away at the church's foundation for so long, and sought to reverse the process, to shake up the hierarchy, to cleanse the wounds that had been dripping with gangrenous infections for hundreds of years. Then he himself was the victim of an assassination attempt, but an unsuccessful one, an attempt blamed on Muslim terrorists—but these dupes did not hatch the plot; they would never have gone that far on their own.

They were only the hired guns, nothing more.

One day, alerted by references to it in a very old file that he happened upon, the new pope found the journal so long hidden. He found it, and read it, and prayed for wisdom.

And then he burned it, the old, old pages quickly turning to ash, as he threw his head back, and screamed, "Lord, Lord, only with Thy strength, only with Thy might can this battle be won."

A battle, yes, a battle for the soul of the Roman Catholic Church. Which may yet be won. The men who burned Joan of Arc at the stake were succeeded, later, by those who were at the forefront of the crusade against the murder of unborn infants.

(My master groans at this turn of events; I secretly rejoice.)

And it continues. This battle. It continues in the Vatican and every archdiocese on the face of Planet Earth.

Flames without end.

The lake of fire stretching in every direction for as far as I can see.

But burning in agony for eternity is not to be the totality of our destiny.

Reliving the past.

That is another part of our punishment, the past and everything it had ever contained.

For a demon, that is Hell indeed.

Especially when I remember the children . . . .

My third child was thus deposited in a foundling
home just like the first two, and I did the same with
the two following: I had five in all. This arrangement
seemed to me so good, so sensible, so appropriate, that
if I did not boast of it publicly it was solely out of
regard for their mother. . . . In a word, I made no secret
of my action . . . because in fact I saw no wrong in it.

—Jean-Jacques Rousseau

Children had been a special target of Satan's for a very long time. He seemed so singularly *devoted* to bringing about their corruption that it could be said with absolute truth that no other group elicited such venomous dedication on his part.

"Be sure you quote me properly," he said at the very beginning of all this. "Be sure you set down every syllable without the slightest error."

"And what is it that you want me to say, master?" I asked.

"They must be attacked at every turn. We can go in so many different directions. But whatever we do, it has to be effective. Destroy the children of any given generation and you rob all other generations to come."

He was standing on the outskirts of Eden or, rather, where Eden had been. There was nothing left now, only straggly weeds, burnt tree stumps, a dry river bed, and bodies, so many bodies, of fish and birds and other creatures—death where there had been nothing of the kind, death replacing the sweet odors and beautiful sounds with its own abysmal scents of filthy decay and that cold silence, except for the shrieking of a wind so forlorn that it seemed to have come straight from Hades.

. . . so many different directions.

Child abandonment was one. There was a period in the first century after the death, burial, and resurrection of Christ when this practice was so widespread that the church fathers sought to counter it in a number of ways. But they tended to fail rather than succeed because Christianity then was not nearly as influential in prodding the public's conscience as it would become later.

"We send them into the cold streets on feet of despair and rejection," Satan was saying, as I returned abruptly from my private thoughts. "They drift into crime. They become diseased. They cry out their anger but few hear them, few care, and they die in physical pain and the deepest emotional anguish. *It is perfect, Observer, perfect!*"

He planned to initiate this during the onslaught of the Roman Empire and continue through to what would be known as the "Middle Ages" and beyond.

"We were so successful for hundreds of years," Satan would say later in retrospect.

And he was.

There was a point, for a century or so after the birth of Christ, at which the business of prostitution went into a prolonged slump—not because of any sudden surge in moral values but, rather, the knowledge that a swelling percentage of abandoned young girls got work at brothels, staying there for a number of years, which raised the danger that men frequenting such places could quite conceivably end up having an evening of sex with their own daughters without ever recognizing the heavily painted "lady"!

This sometimes casual rejection of children by their flesh-and-blood parents went on for many centuries, all the while my master rejoicing in the misery of those countless numbers of children cast out into the streets of the cities of the then-civilized world. From Rome to Paris to London and elsewhere, the little ones mostly starved to death if they did not become creatures of the night's dark alleys and dirty streets, their bodies available to anyone who could pay for their services by giving them money or food or simple shelter, or else they would, in the awful weather of winter, freeze where they dropped.

Oh, how hard it was to stand there, as they died so slowly, as they became aware of my presence, reaching out their small pale hands toward me, their bloodshot eyes begging, always begging, afraid of the greater darkness that was sweeping inexorably over them.

But in the midst of that ravenous evil pleasure of his, Satan had not anticipated the manner in which God would intervene. His demonic nature had been absorbed so long without seeming rebuke in what he was inflicting on the pitiable innocent through the sin-nurtured insensitivity of their earthly parents and the blindness inherent in the society of those ignorant times—indeed, he assumed that he somehow could go on and on unimpeded, as though God could not see, did not care.

It all happened through the mere kindness of strangers.

How those words skewered the plans upon which Satan had spent so much effort implementing!

. . . the kindness of strangers.

After celebrating for so long the mean-spiritedness of a vast majority of mankind, he was unprepared for other than the most sporadic and tentative acts of concern. The change commenced with the first few hospices, foundling hospitals, and orphanages—many of these, especially the latter, imperfect at best, often operated haphazardly, but still not the streets, still not the streets.

More and more of these sprung up as ecclesiastical and civic organizations came into existence for the express purpose of assisting the poor and the homeless. An example was the Hospital of St. John set up in Jerusalem and staffed entirely by Western Europeans—its sole purpose: caring for abandoned or, as they called them in those days, "exposed" children.

For a time, the number of cases of children thrown out of their homes actually increased because parents could deposit their offspring on the doorsteps of these institutions and not be afflicted quite so severely with attacks of guilt or "conscience," since they had the assurance that helpless boys and girls were not automatically being condemned to death.

But the Christian sensibilities that made better care of such children inevitable also led to stricter penalties against the abandoning parents. Finally there were not only fewer cases but better treatment of those that did occur.

So, Satan gave up for hundreds of years, and turned his attention elsewhere.

But then the latter half of the twentieth century presented him with new opportunities. Drugs were introduced to such an extent that hundreds of thousands of young people experimented casually, or so they rationalized, then became hooked, with some addicts as young as nine years of age. He was able to generate a whole industry dealing in child pornography, and he got special satisfaction in this area.

"It is a slow form of death," he told me as he watched three children expose themselves in front of a 16 millimeter movie camera. "We destroy their minds, and they begin a long period of suffering, then they move out into society and explode their frustrations on others. Perfect, Observer, as perfect as can be!"

He was right, of course; but such measures of pure evil all were eclipsed by the one that was his proudest accomplishment, if pride can be considered the right word.

Abortion.

It pleased him for a variety of reasons. First, tens of millions of babies were condemned to death—but many would be born alive, only to be strangled in minutes or else nursed back to health and sold out the back doors of numerous abortion clinics to couples so desperate for children that they wouldn't hesitate to go the black market route. Second, abortion would divide a nation, pitting the pro-choice adherents against the pro-lifers. And third, ah, yes, this was a stroke of genius on Satan's part.

"If they only knew what would happen when they finally *want* to have children," he said. "So few understand the fate their actions force upon the babies which are next in line."

I nodded in reluctant understanding, knowing that there was a 40-60 percent greater chance for mothers with a previous abortion to give birth to a retarded child or a child afflicted with blood, bone, or other diseases.

To the delight of my master, to the delight of the entire demonkind....

It was on such occasions, among many, when revulsion welled up most violently within me. There I was, watching, chronicling, lending support by my silence. But what good, I told myself, was it to say anything, anything at all? My words would have no impact whatever on the master; he could ignore me with impunity. I was hardly a threat. And yet there was no way that I could turn back to Almighty God, no way He would accept me if I did because my rebellion was unforgiveable, and, therefore, I was without hope, hope reserved only for those human beings who accepted His Son into their lives as their Savior, their Lord.

So I would always be by Satan's side, giving him my allegiance, having to take down every word, every raving, every blasphemy, and constantly reaffirming my loyalty—for he is in need of that, craving those moments when I am at his feet, looking up into his eyes, telling him the sweetest words, the most beautiful compliments, pledging that I will follow him forever, even when he asks me every so often to put my book down and do a special favor for him, and I have to step out of the role of Observer, and become D'Evel. D'Evel convinces himself that if he didn't do it, someone else will, and D'Evel does what the master wants, deeds as sick as anything Mifult and others have ever dirtied themselves with, especially that time he demanded, "Words, words, only words, give me *deeds*!"

I am driven to perhaps the foulest moment of my existence, the slaughter of missionaries in a Central American country, and every member of their families. I plotted their ambush through my rebel surrogates, making the missionaries think they were on a mission of peace, whereas they were being led to their doom.

I stand in the midst of their dying, falling bodies, as they see me just before their souls ascend. There is this one lovely little girl, her blonde hair stained red, looking at me not with hatred, not with fear, none of that as she has *every* right to do— for I have egged on her murderers, driving them to the monstrous carnage—yet she has nothing but pity on that sweet, sweet face. Oh, how can she feel that way about me, how can she ever, ever, ever be so forgiving, so very forgiving?

And I have to admit something quite ghastly to myself. I have to admit that I enjoyed that massacre, that the satisfaction it stirs within me was pervasive, that I wanted to go and find others, and have their lives, their earthly, mortal lives torn from them, and watch the pain they endured as this happened.

No, this cannot be! I am not like that. Throughout history that is what I have told myself.

But in that moment, the ground soaked in blood, cries filling the air, I realize the truth, yet this truth does not set me free; it entombs me with the suffocating realization that I am not so different, not so different from my demon brethren after all.

Then I return to Satan, and tell him what I have done, and as he congratulates me with fervor, I pick up my book and become obedient Observer, the stench of shed blood fading quickly enough.

Or has it, ever?

*D*uring the Civil War, I had a plantation owner as my host. He treated his slaves abominally. The men he beat, some of the pretty women he raped. Eventually he lost everything. Eventually the slaves were freed. Some of them wanted to kill their former owner. They went so far as to tie a rope around his neck, and were about to hang him from a large oak tree.

One of them spoke up.

"No!" he said. "It must not be."

"But why?" another asked. "He has been very cruel. He has violated our women folk. What mercy does he deserve?"

"He deserves none," a third added.

The rest shouted in agreement.

"*That* is why we have to show mercy," the one former slave continued. "None of *us* deserves even the slightest mercy."

His comrades did not understand.

He then grabbed an old banjo and started playing it as he sang:

'Twas I that shed the sacred blood;
I nailed Him to the tree;
I crucified the Christ of God;
I joined the mockery.

Of all that shouting multitude
I feel that I am one;
And in that din of voices rude
I recognize my own.

Around the cross the throng I see,
Mocking the Sufferer's groan;
Yet still my voice it seems to be,
As if I mocked alone.

The words came out a little differently than that; he pronounced them all with the thick accent of his people at that time. But that was the message that came through.

That hymn had the deepest impact. Several of the men broke out in tears, so moved were they.

Two immediately went and cut the rope, and took the owner and salved his cuts and bruises, and washed him down, and gave him food.

I could not stay, of course.

The Holy Spirit took up residence within that white man, and I was chased out, as always it is so.

I looked back at him, at the blacks who had been his slaves. I looked back further than that, to the Cross of Calvary.

Yet still my voice—

Someone else sang, but the words seemed mine alone.

*O*ne of the principal dilemmas I have had across time and space is finding a host whom I could occupy so that my journal can be continued. (After all, I am but spirit and cannot hold a pen or operate a computer or anything of the sort, so I must possess those whose physical presence enables me the means of transcribing all that my master wishes—as well as some thoughts that are mine alone.)

 . . . *that are mine alone.*

How often have I come face-to-face with that issue? When we are in league with Lucifer, is *anything* truly ours and ours alone? If we are so united with him that, in our devotion, we follow him after casting aside the wonders of Heaven, how separate can we be or, rather, are we one and the same?

 . . . *mine alone.*

The images that I take such great pains to have written down through my hapless hosts, are these so private, so personal that they *can* be called *mine*? Or are they merely *his* funneled through me, and then through the flesh-and-blood "house" that I inhabit, onto the papyrus and, yea, many, many centuries later, the computer disk?

It began with Cain after he had murdered Abel, and was forced to run in shame for the rest of his life. (Cain could never be happy, could never know fulfilment, from the moment he shed his brother's blood, and, later, took the lives of others, always falling victim to anger mixed with guilt. Ultimately he gave my master yet another victory by going quite mad, screaming, screaming, screaming until he was cast out into the desert, because he was thought to be possessed by my kind, and died after stumbling into a bed of scorpions.)

There was also Nimrod. And King Saul. Many more after these . . . kings, harlots, centurions, even those among the priesthood of ancient Israel.

And, later, Judas.

Yes, Judas.

(Satan and I indwelt him while DuRong controlled Caiphas, and other fallen brethern extended control throughout the groups of Sadducees and Pharisees, and then Mifult led a thrust into the house of Herod.)

Judas was, as could be imagined, someone in whom my master indeed took special pleasure. He put down everything I ever wanted in my book, with no protest whatever. He was the ideal servant, pursuing infamy while convincing himself of noble intent, trying to force the Messiah's hand, as it were, and get Him to start a war against the Romans, ultimately throwing off their onerous yoke.

Yet, after he hanged himself, Judas became only another link in an infernal chain, and we both left that limp flesh as I moved on to another, and another, my journal always being carried along also.

And with so many others through the centuries following, I labored so that the chain would not be broken, my journal *had* to be complete, and this drove me to the next body, and the one after that.

Generation succeeding generation, again and again, taking over the very being of someone who could be my mouthpiece.

They would put down the words that I spoke to their minds. And they would hide the journal so that none would find it until that grand day of Lucifer's Revenge.

For thousands of years this went on; for thousands of years I abode in the shells of the worst criminals, the most despicable human beings of history. I saw through their eyes as they spilled the blood of those unfortunate enough to be in their way.

I remember Jack the Ripper.

I was there when he murdered his first victim. And the last. I was with him in that hidden place in one of the castles owned by the royal family, where he finally died from one of the sexually-transmitted diseases of that time that I cleverly led him to contract.

Evil people. People for whom it was normal to slice open another human being and, in some cases, take some of the organs—

They were my hosts. I could not touch Florence Nightingale . . . Martin Luther . . . Calvin. Those from whom I could have learned soaring truths, not abysmal lies cloaked in the most repellant corruption. Others had that privilege, the unfallen—not I, chronicler of venality.

On and on, virtually without relief.

Until one day in Auschwitz.

My host was a guard named Hans. He could be counted among the worst, showing actual *pleasure* in kicking prisoners, sending them into the lethal "showers," denying them water when they were thirsty, on and on.

And at night he wrote down these deeds, plus thoughts whose origin even he must have wondered about, thoughts beyond his experience but not mine, never beyond mine.

The latest of many over the centuries.

And not the best.

None of them was best. Was Jack the Ripper best, perhaps the lesser evil because his victims could be counted on the fingers of both hands and didn't require a computer printout? Was the cruel feudal lord in the nightmarish period of European plague best because he didn't *directly* plunge a dagger into an innocent heart but simply denied mercy? Was the modern robber baron who bilked a large savings and loan association out of tens of millions the best because no one *died* at his hand?

The lesser of evils?

Could *anything* or *anyone* be called that? *All* evil was part of the master's plan, all who practiced it manifested one aspect or another of his personality.

For Hans, the Auschwitz extermination camp was his private hell, over which he presided as a master.

Until one day. . . .

That moment, one so dreaded by Satan, one that would continue to aggrieve him mightily in the years to follow, that moment when he lost the body and soul of Hans forever. . . .

It came as Hans was dragging a nearly naked woman behind one of the barracks. His intention was to sexually abuse her. Other guards saw what was happening, and smiled, or laughed, as they walked by, one of them shouting, "Grab some for me, Hans!"

"I will!" Hans assured him as he slapped the Jewess across the cheek, and tore at what was left of her garment.

Suddenly she stopped struggling, *so* suddenly that he looked at her with some concern, thinking that she had died in that instant.

She was still alive under him, unmoving.

Her face!

The eyes seemed to be shining as though the sun were reflecting off them. There was a faint smile curling up the sides of her lips.

"You *mock* me!" he growled.

She spoke then, words he would never forget.

"Mock you, sir? I do not mock you at all. I was praying to my dear Lord about you. And He answered me, in my spirit.

That is what my countenance shows—joy over your coming salvation!"

He struck her again and again but still he could not wipe that expression from her face. Finally he stood, grabbed his rifle, and hit her in the chest with its butt, and she fell to the ground. He stood over her, intending to kick her several times with his hob-nailed boot.

"I forgive you, Hans," she whispered, pain apparent in her voice. "I forgive you and—"

His heavy boot smashed into her hip once, twice, a third time as he kept saying, "Goddam Jew, goddam Jew, goddam Jew," over and over.

Her joy seemed stronger than ever!

"No, Hans, God does *not* damn me, my brother," she said. "Nor will He damn you. As one who has accepted His Son as my Savior and my Lord, I will stand at the very gates of Heaven someday as you enter, and, with my hand in yours, we will walk the golden streets together."

He was about to blow her head to pieces with his luger when another guard stopped him.

"Don't, Hans," he said. "Give her to Mengele. He could use her, I wager. Don't take individual responsibility. Let the butcher do it." (Even the SS thought of Josef Mengele in that manner, either with admiration or disgust!)

Hans nodded. The other guard picked her up and carried her in the direction of the labs.

That evening Hans went to a nearby beer parlor with several of the other guards and started to get drunk.

"Good for you, Hans," one of them said in congratulation. "One less Jew whore to have to watch over after Mengele gets done with his scissors and his knives and whatever he'll do to her."

"She wasn't a whore," he said abruptly. "She was a virgin."

"You had her first then! Let's all drink to Hans' finest conquest, and may he have many more like her. Love them first, then leave them for the mad doctor! That's Hans for you."

Hans stood, and put all three hundred pounds of his weight into his fist as he smashed the other guard, who sailed clear across the smoke-filled parlor. Then he glowered at the others, and stalked outside.

. . . we will walk the golden streets together.

He spit on the dirt at his feet as he remembered those words.

"Jew lies!" he shouted. "There is no God! If there were a God, how could He allow scum like me to exist?"

Hans tried to forget the woman, her words, that look, the very idea that she could have genuinely forgiven him. But her image stayed with him, taunting him in the middle of the night, robbing him of sleep and, during the day, of appetite.

Days passed. His behavior, if anything, grew worse toward the other prisoners at Auschwitz. Even his fellow guards noticed this.

Finally, toward evening, nearly a week after his encounter with the Jewess, he was prepared to go off his shift when an odd thought seized him—indeed compulsion might be a better word—odd because of the man Hans was, a "pure" SS guard who had been taught to view Jews as vermin, and the collected masses of them at Auschwitz as diseased cattle.

He had to *know* what had happened to her!

No one had ever before forgiven him for anything. He had to know her fate. This need would not loosen its grip on him.

So he headed toward the labs, at an hour when he knew they would be closed down.

No! I screamed in his ear, afraid of what he would find. *You mustn't. Let her alone! Forget her—she's just one contemptible Jewess.*

But he ignored my inner voice, perceived more than heard, and managed to gain entrance through a rear window that was half-open.

He had a flashlight, its beam cast upon cages with human beings in them instead of animals, beds with chained men and women, jars filled with—

Hans came to a large tank in the middle of that particular room. It was quite tall, metallic, the top rim nearly two feet above his head. He pulled a nearby ladder over to it, and started to climb the rungs. As he neared the top, he placed two hands over the edge, and pulled back immediately.

So cold!

The chill rippled throughout his entire body.

Then he could see over the edge.

Several bodies were floating in the chill water, all naked. He examined them, not recognizing three, but the fourth, yea, her flesh nearly blue, he saw the Jewess; somehow she was not quite dead, her eyelids flickering briefly, her gaze meeting his own, and she smiled, smiled in recognition, her lips moving silently, but somehow it was as though he heard the words anyway.

I shall enter Heaven soon, past those gates. For you it will be a while but it will be. . . .

He fell off the ladder, then got to his feet, and hurried back to that window, and climbed through it, and then stopped, shaking, telling himself no one else must find out, no one must ever know.

He tried to pretend that all was normal with him, tried to put up a front of business-as-usual. But he couldn't. Nothing would ever be *normal* with him again.

The next day, during a break, he walked back toward the labs, saw bodies being dumped into a cart, and taken to the crematoriums. In a short while the ashes would be disposed of on the outskirts of the camp, a spot he knew only too well, having been assigned periodically to the burial detail.

He tried to pretend that he wouldn't be drawn to that place, tried, yes, mightily so, but failed, and found himself returning to the spot where the Jewess' ashes had been dumped, then covered over with dirt. He would stand there for a few minutes, then leave, and not come back for a day or two, then stay another hour, then leave; finally he would remain for a long time, sitting on the ground, and eventually talking not so much to himself but in a sense to her.

"How could you react as you did?" he would ask. "How could you treat me with such forgiveness?"

Finally, after repeating that question, in one form or another, he would start to weep, then stop abruptly, ashamed of the emotion that engulfed him, his Aryan conditioning kicking in to cut off the tears, the tears that should never be shed in the first place, but certainly not over a Jewess.

My master sent K'Rupt to harden the guard named Hans. Normally K'Rupt did his job quite well. But this time it was different. This time—

Hans changed.

Hans changed most dramatically the next time he went to that same spot, and unable to stand the guilt any longer, took a shovel and dug up the earth. He found more than just her ashes, of course, found deep, awful piles of it from countless other Jews and gypsies and other enemies of Aryan purity and opponents of their merciless domination, running his hands through the white and gray flakes, thin, sharp pieces of bone cutting his fingers and palms . . . then the tiny little testament, at first not sure of what it was, the print so small. He sat there in the midst of that mass grave, reading the words, sobbing, first enraged at his weakness, nearly throwing the little square booklet away but stopping himself and reading further, finally climbing out of that grave, and leaving that scene, not back to the camp, not there at all, but away, in the countryside, walking for miles. They hunted for him but he was gone, and no one had any idea what had happened.

I was in that body of his, for a brief while longer, and then I had to leave. The Holy Spirit entered, the Holy Spirit came in at Hans' invitation as the now former guard of Auschwitz knelt in a farmer's field many miles from the camp. For an instant we confronted one another, as a struggle swept on in Hans' soul.

"You must leave," He told me.

"Yes, I know, Stedfast," I replied. "But I must be concerned about who will next take over the penning of my book. You know about my book, do you not?"

He looked sadly at me, nodding as He did.

"Is that all you think there is to it, Observer? You do not realize the truth, do you? The truth about your book?"

I was deeply puzzled by what He said but let those words pass by as though never spoken.

"It is all I have, my only purpose," I said, "transcribing what I must so that the master will have a record of everything."

"Then why do you leave, Observer?" the Holy Spirit asked. "Is not your work so innocent?"

"Because the Holy Spirit and the Devil cannot co-inhabit the same—" I replied from memory.

I cut myself off. Understanding invaded my mind.

"You and Satan are as one," the Holy Spirit said, not with triumph, rather the deepest regret to which I had witnessed. "You do what you do for him, in slavery to his every whim, and yet count that as nothing. To be silent in the face of evil is to be evil yourself, as you have been since the beginning when you turned your back on all that was holy. But you go beyond mere acquiescence, and cooperate with evil, recording it for your master, and yet you claim no choice in the matter. In one way you are *worse* than he who is what he is and makes no pretense about it. But to all his sins must be added your own, that hypocrisy with which you try to cloak the willing synergy between the two of you over the ages in a façade of innocence."

He spoke now with a touch of weariness.

"Past the lips of *any* being, human or demon, such words as come through your protestations are like roses that soldiers put in their muskets on holidays."

He looked at me with an intensity that I could not long abide.

"That was written a hundred years ago," the Holy Spirit added, "but it will remain true until the end of time."

And there I stood, as Hans walked toward the farmhouse directly ahead, where he came upon a Christian family that welcomed him, and to whom he poured out his thoughts, his emotions, and found the kind husband and wife accepting him as cleansed. (I knew it would be quite wearisome for him in the weeks to come, as he repeatedly confronted his guilt over the acts that had been committed, but now that he had accepted Christ into his life as Savior and Lord, he had the promise of relief, freedom from the crushing burden that otherwise would have been his until the day he died—though so few of the SS admitted that they suffered from anything of the sort, instead trying to wash the guilt away in an alcoholic haze, or deaden it through ever more barbaric actions.)

I saw myself in Hans as he poured out his inner self to those strangers, feeling freer to do so with them than he had ever imagined possible because there was *so much* bottled up inside him, previously hidden behind that mask of Nazi hardness, Nazi training that attempted to squeeze out any vestiges of compassion for any other human being, enabling them to do what they were told was necessary for the glory of the fatherland. For me, it was not Hitler but Satan, and the fatherland was to be that over which his coming campaign would make him supreme ruler. But for me there was never to be purging as with Hans, for I had no one, stranger or friend, to whom I could turn in such moments of vulnerability.

I lingered as long as I could outside that modest little home, listening to the three of them. And then I returned to my book.

It was sprawled on the dirt of that field, a slight breeze ruffling the pages.

Who would be next? Who would go by that I might overtake them and enter uninvited?

A teenage boy on his bicycle, a scruffy-looking lad. Yes, yes! Satan would be pleased.

I approached him but stepped back. He was humming a hymn as he went on past. (I realize, of course, that this in itself was not a firm indication of his spiritual state, but it was unusual enough, in that war period, to give at least a hint. Young people then could hardly be expected to be humming such a tune alone, though they might have done so with others around in order to create some favorable impression in those who would be hearing them. Forty years later, if he was singing something from a heavy metal album, there would have been no doubt in my mind about the feasibility of gaining entrance to his soul.)

A short while later, a Gestapo agent stopped on the road for a moment. Then he got out of his car and ran into the field. With no emotion whatever, he removed his gun from its holster and shot himself in the temple. (That was probably the work of D'Guilt, though he had always had a hard time with *anyone* in the Gestapo.)

Next came two ministers, both on bicycles. They stopped for a bit, and sat down on the grass and talked, and talked.

The short one, younger, was talking about whether the Bible merely *contained* the Word of God or was, from cover to cover, His Word in every respect.

The older one, taller, a bit plump, took a stand in favor of the Bible *as* God's Word, whereas the other argued against this, citing all the potential for error of translation and transcription over the centuries.

After perhaps an hour they ended the discussion, and the older minister left. The younger one lingered a bit, inhaling the vegetation-scented air. As he was about to leave, he noticed that current portion of my journal lying there. With some curiosity, he walked over to it, picked it up, and idly leafed through the pages.

He took both of us home with him.

I think perhaps the very worst part of being what I am is that I can communicate best just with others of my kind, for they are my only true companions.

My companions. . . .

I should think of them with affection, but how can I do that? Love is not really in our vocabulary, you know. Satan thinks hate, talks hate, practices hate. The only love he has is for himself.

How can you feel even a touch of love, a suggestion of it, ersatz love or otherwise—how can you say you love a creature that inhabits a human being who is sucking a baby out of its mother's womb, limb by limb, bits-and-pieces of fingers and toes, a tiny, tiny skull, fragments of skin, and blood, blood that flows in a *thing* that is supposed to be nothing more than mush, like cereal in a bowl in the morning?

The answer is that no real emotion exists between us, except what is born of the necessity of our circumstance. We tolerate one another. We come to one another with the burden of our multiplying iniquities, and sometimes there *is* temporary

68

relief, a momentary cessation of pain continual—but then it is gone, and we are back where we have always been, chained to a creature with whom we have felt less and less rapport.

There is Mifult, for example, the demon principally responsible for abortions as well as other forms of the abuse of the young. He certainly has been successful over the years, especially the past twenty or so, successful in corrupting the minds and the souls of those who favor this butchery.

"I have just seen Darien," Mifult says to me this very afternoon.

Darien on his journey down Angelwalk, the path he has been trodding as he searches for Satan, trying to piece together the puzzle of his own outlook, about the master, about the Casting Out, and so much more besides.

"And what happened?" I ask.

"He got to me, Observer."

We are standing near a man who is tossing fetuses, limp, bloody fetuses, into a plastic trash bag.

"I had to admit my dream to him," Mifult tells me.

Ah, yes, Mifult's dream . . . .

"I am very much alone on a plain. It is totally barren—only sand as far as I can see. Suddenly I notice some specks at the horizon. They seem to be moving, though they are still too far away for me to be sure.

"I wait. Closer they come. I begin to see forms, of different sizes. Still closer. They are now near enough so that I can see what those forms are.

"Babies, and little children. Hordes of them. Almost like bees from a distant hive. There may be thousands, or more, forming a long line extending all the way from the horizon. They surround me.

"One of them approaches, holding out her hand. She says, 'Mister, why did you do those terrible things to me?' And I realize she has been the victim of a child molester.

"A boy comes up, his body covered with bruises. Others as well. Suddenly the crowd parts and I see the most devastating image of all: a tiny body, its arms and legs missing, somehow rolling, rolling,

*rolling toward me, crying, stopping at my feet. His head is turned
toward me, the eyes pleading, the skin wrinkled and blotched and
smelling, oh God, smelling of saline solution. The first attempt had
failed, so he was pulled apart limb by limb.*

"*I run. I run as fast as I can. Abruptly I fall and lose
consciousness. I think I come to again, but I am not sure. Suddenly
I feel someone tearing at me. There is intense pain. Then more
pain. I scream out. But there is no response. I try desperately to fight
against someone who is pulling at me, but I realize, I realize, I
realize that I have no arms, no legs.*

"*The next instant I am at someone's feet. Looking up.
Pleading. I have become that baby—*"

It is always the final words that are the most compelling,
perhaps the most shocking from Mifult's recollection of his
nightmare.

"*and—I—am—looking—up—at—myself!*"*

"You told Darien everything?" I ask.

"I did," Mifult replies.

"The master will be displeased."

Mifult nods.

Concede nothing to the enemy—a precept of warfare—
and no less so in the spiritual realm.

But Mifult did just that. He admitted the pain of what he
was doing, within himself and within his victim, but even that
was not the worst part of it. The worst was that he admitted to
a wandering unfallen angel that there *were* victims at all. He
swept away in an instant a major tenet of a carefully orchestrated
campaign to *encourage* abortion by the attempted removal of
guilt. How can there *be* guilt over blobs of flesh, lumps of skin
and bone, and all the insignificant rest? No need to get all
worked up over *that*!

Mifult is increasingly typical of the rest of us, those who can
no longer bury their consciences in the adulation that brought
about our state in the first place.

And yet, sadly, *some* are more than ever like the master,
more than ever zealous in their pursuits, more than ever *eager*

to wash their hands, as it were, in the flowing rivers of blood that have been spilled by my kind through the ages. They have stood in the very center of many battlefields, gaining *pleasure* as they walk over the spilled guts that come from victor and vanquished alike, grenades or lances or bullets or cannon balls tearing the wounded and the dying open to cries of agony.

"I'm afraid," the man will say. "I don't want to go to Hell."

"But *Hell* is where you are bound," the demons will respond, "where *we* will have you forever."

"Oh, *no!*"

"Yes, yes, *yes!*" a creature of stench and decay will shout back as that human soul leaves that now limp and superfluous body, reaching out for the latest victim—*only* the latest, for countless others are ready for the line, *their* turn decreed by *their* sin because there has been no forgiveness, no cleansing for the simple reason that there has been no acceptance of the One Who could change it all.

*T*here is no way I can enjoy any sustained contact with that which is noble and beauteous and uplifting, except through chance encounters perhaps, with Darien or Stedfast or another like them—at least contact in the sense of some form of symbiosis, as when a man sees a beautiful woman, and the two fall in love and there is a merging of mind and body and future in marriage. Any marriage of any kind is beyond my reach, merely something to look at when I am with human beings, if you can ever call what I do, what I am, if you can call any of it being *with* them. . . . I look at them as they touch one another, as they hold one another, as they share the feeling between themselves, as—

The unfallen angels have such a state with God their Creator. They and He are undivided. They are, in some indefinable way, extensions of His divinity, not as the members of the Trinity but as human lovers, separate but yet bound together by the way they think, feel or act with each other.

And to what or with whom are demons bound? To a God who inspires? That is not our destiny, perhaps it never was.

Did God know?

As the omniscient One, was it that He knew in advance of our coming rebellion? Was that why I have such a strong memory of Him watching us leave His Heaven by the thousands, and there being sorrow in His countenance—but not surprise, not puzzlement, not utter amazement that we would elect to follow a different master?

All of us left with anticipation, throwing off the shackles of what had come to be, for us in our delusion, oppressive goodness and purity, which carried with them the necessity of total obedience if we were to have continued in His presence.

Satan could no longer tolerate living in the presence of One greater than himself. That was the basis for his rebellion, and yet in time that very statement itself changed, *had* to change, because if Satan continued to acknowledge that God indeed was the master, not he, this would mean that Satan himself was the servant, and how could he have abided this demeaning estate for time and eternity?

So he nurtured the true conceit of his existence, a conceit which he was far less successful instilling in us, the conceit that made him think he was in fact *greater* than God, that the feeling of being less than Him was a trick, a trick perpetrated by God to ensure eternal subservience.

"I will not be fooled," Satan bellowed, and he repeated this a hundred times, a thousand times, countless, countless times until he came to believe the lie himself. It was a statement always there, reinforced by those fools among mankind who have convinced themselves that there is no God simply because they have convinced themselves that there is no God.

I speak, therefore I am.

I said it, therefore it is.

Many a deceived soul has stood outside and waved a fist at the sky and said, "If You really are there, strike me dead, now, for daring to doubt first Your magnificence, then Your justice, and, yes, today, this very moment, the very fact that You *are*!"

And when they have been allowed to live, when God *seems* not to have responded, their defiance is justified in their own minds. And they go on to delude others, not realizing that perhaps they are, in the short term, free of God, as they would put it, but assuredly enslaved to *my* master who then has become *theirs* as well.

For some, wealth is a substitute, and along with it, the power that wealth invariably brings. For others, it is fame. For *all*, there *is* a substitute of *some* kind, taking the seat of the throne of their lives.

But God does intervene. God can take the wealth, the power, the fame of that celebrated New England family and show the actual poverty of their lives by the persistent interpolation of tragedy—the losses of loved ones, the scent of scandal drawing the rumor-mongers to them as ravenous vultures to a pile of dead meat, bleeding and bare and already in the process of decay.

Your idol is shattered in the dust to prove that God's dust is greater than your idol.

Words read and not forgotten, words heavy with true truth.

For such as this family, placing so much faith in its bank accounts and its political connections, the idols do fall, do break into irreparable pieces, do lie there in the dust, *as* the dust, mocking in their brokenness, as though crying out from the shards of what they once were, "Stupid one, stupid one that you are, see what it has gotten you!"

I t is true that I can go anywhere I want, in the twinkling of an eye, from the Amazon to the Indian Ocean; from the streets of London to the outback of Australia; from today to yesterday; from prehistoric caves to ultra-modern skyscrapers. I am not captive to time or place but still I am a prisoner, though there are no bars, no confining barbed wire. I am a prisoner of my insubstantial spiritual state.

Sometimes, as I have said before, I will see the Others, those once my comrades in Heaven but now my eternal enemies.

Enemies. . . .

I wonder periodically how that could be, how it could *ever* be. I tremble at what has changed, what has changed indeed, since I remember so very well what it was like in my former home. And, of course, so does Lucifer, once the finest, the most beautiful of all angels.

He remembers, as we all do, the absence of death, disease, pain, the *reality* of joy, peace, and that indescribable, sublime fulfilment of being in the presence of our Holy Creator.

Our Creator.

Not even Satan has forgotten that singular fact. Without Him, we would not exist.

God gave us life, blessed life. . . .

What have we done with this gift?

We have thrown it back in His face again and again. We have turned beauty into corrupted countenance after countenance.

And what *is* that countenance? If a mirror could offer our reflection, surely that sight alone would mean the end of any hold we have on sinners the world over. That is what I say now, but then I am probably wrong, for there are those still intent on worshiping evil whatever the face. Yet many, many indeed, seeing the reality of what we are, *would* shrink in fear and loathing, turning away forever.

We all have become images of Satan, just as we commenced life in the image of God. In Satan we see ourselves and we recoil—but it is the disgust of a drug addict as he jabs yet another needle into yet another vein, hating what he is doing but not able to mitigate the addiction—and after however long, he is frequently headed for Skid Row where many have been chained to drugs or alcohol or both for a very long time, their bodies battered and sick shells for souls that long for the relief they assume comes through death, not realizing that, without salvation through Christ, they yearn for something more awful than a lifetime of Skid Rows.

We are will-of-the-wisp vagrants, lost and lonely nonentities who wander from place to place, meeting often in cemeteries among the worm-infested remnants of our mad deeds—but just as frequently in great and grand buildings littered with the consequences of hypocrisy, men and women stumbling about month after month, year after year, leading others astray as our surrogates among the ripe fields ready for harvest.

*A*nd what is the fruit of the Others as they approach the harvest of God?

It is St. Francis taking off the rich garments of his ancestry and putting on the rags of his obedience. It is a bowl of food to a starving child in a desert land. It is peace between enemies, a white hand joined with a black one raised before Him in a chorus of praise as *our* bigotry, as *our* violence, as *our* fruits are shed like the profane encumbrances they are. It is wounds healed, pain stopped. It is a baby being born, not a fetus terminated. It is all this and a vast tapestry of other people, acts, moments.

Though my kind is loathe to admit it, we do look at what we see in *their* wake and know that we have chosen wrongly. In comparison to ourselves and our malignant deeds, the Others truly are pure, clean, kind, and good, without the slightest taint of selfishness or despair.

But their kindness, their goodness, has been translated beyond thought and deposition into deeds; there is so much that is noble and decent for which they have been responsible, working under the direction of the Holy Spirit.

I think of Stedfast, who is the source of the legend about a guardian angel. He was with Darien every step of my former comrade's odyssey along Angelwalk. Darien was never aware; God kept Stedfast's presence a mystery. Darien was never in any real danger; it was just that he had to find out the reality of what my master was all about, as humans often say about another.

Stedfast.

I have seen him usually from a distance since the Casting Out. I have seen him by the side of Mother Teresa, encouraging her, aiding the Holy Spirit.

Stedfast has been with redeemed men and women as they walked up wooden steps to the guillotine.

He has held the hand of Joan of Arc amidst the flames.

He has been with the homeless.

He has turned away legions of demons as they tried to wreck the lives of countless millions over the centuries. He has been the Holy Spirit's dutiful, steadfast lieutenant. He has done it all out of love for the Father.

To serve such a One who can inspire such devotion!

All that I am yearns for what they have, what they can do, the joy they bring, the peace.

They can leave Heaven, they can return, they can—

See the smile of a Holy God.

God smiles, God cries, God gets angry.

He smiled often when we were there, my kind and I. Back then there were no tears, no anger.

We—

I hold the words for a brief moment—and then they gush out, through my host of the moment onto solid paper through real ink, born from the invisible presence of myself.

We made God cry. We made God angry. We did this, the master, all of us. . . .

And that is why we suffer. As suffer we should.

Because of us, Hell is.

A round table.
Hands on top, palms down.
People with their eyes closed, heads tilted slightly backward.
A medium chanting.
Calling up the spirits.
—Shall I pose as the father this time?
—No, you should be the daughter. You were the father during the last seance.

It has been astonishing to me how *many* human beings are so eager to make contact with us, so willing to open themselves up to what they feel my master can offer.

I suspect that untold millions of people the world over who worship Satan in one form or another imagine they would be ecstatic if they could only *be* one of us, exercising the so-called powers they envision us to possess.

If they could only be one of us. . . .

And what would they become if that were the case?

The wielders of power?

Yea, they would have it, and a great deal else indeed. They would have the power to plunge kingdoms into darkness and despair by corrupting the men who rule them.

They would have the power to cause voyeurs to ogle naked bodies in dark little rooms smelling of sweat, their eyes pressed against viewing machines with flickering images on their pupils, and a slot for the next quarter of a dollar.

They would be able to precipitate needless death after death, whether on the battlefield, or in dirty alleys, or in clinics founded for healing but turned over to slaughter riding on the twin backs of vanity and convenience.

And what more would there be for the ones running after us with slavering anticipation?

No sickness. No death.

Life eternal, life about which they need never fear that it was running out.

And they would have a leader, a *real* leader, one with single-mindedness of purpose, dedication.

They would never have to sleep. Or eat. And they would be witness to *all* the monumental events of all the years of history on this planet named Earth.

I have known archaelogists who would have given us their souls to be in the midst of Ancient Rome—not walking through its ruins, but through the thriving city itself.

Or with the Mayans or the Aztecs or the Incas when *their* civilizations were flourishing.

But not just archaelogists, of course. There were the historians who would have thought it truly Heaven to meet Caesar in the flesh, to be in Queen Victoria's court, to hear Lincoln give the Gettysburg Address.

Archaeologists and historians and others who would lust after the possibilities, the many enticing possibilities that could be realized by being eternal, by wandering the planet with us.

And artists who would have been delirious with joy to watch Michelangelo actually painting the ceiling of the Sistine

Chapel rather than just observe the faded centuries-old images
to which they had to be resigned as mere mortals.

Or supposedly mad Van Gogh with his masterpieces. Or
Raphael. Or—

I reconsider Van Gogh, knowing all too intimately that it
was not madness at all with this man, it was me inside him, the
artist acting as my host, my presence a deterrent, and how I
wanted to leave, how I wanted to let his genius flower fully
without that deranged edge to it, and yet I could not, I could
not leave because I was there at the assignment of my master,
and I could not disobey him.

We have been with them all, the geniuses of mankind, the
madmen. We have been witness to everything glorious of which
they were capable as well as the debased side of their lives—
Michelangelo's homosexual liasons and Van Gogh's promiscuous heterosexuality, about which my kind have mounted propaganda over the centuries since such artists have practiced their
art, propaganda that uses these men to legitimatize that prof-
ligate nature they manifested resoundingly, saying in words so
nice, so respectable, so logical, "How can you condemn men
like these? Look at what they were capable of!"

Some fell for that—nay, *many* did—nay again, *most* of
mankind, aware of the Michelangelos and the Van Goghs and
others, assumed that genius, surpassing as it was with these
men, the product of that genius inspiring people for centuries,
that genius, whether they realized they were proclaiming this or
not, evidenced a kind of de facto salvation for them, as they
assumed that the divine images in the Vatican could only be of
God, and that God alone was with Michelangelo when he did
his work.

But then if images were tacit acknowledgment of the
salvation of their artist-creator, surely all the statues in all the
churches in all the countries on this troubled planet would lead
onlookers to proclaim that there was no such thing as an artist
or a sculptor of Christian scenes or figures who was *ever* anything
but a saintly, utterly holy and saved individual.

And there is something else. As a consequence, couldn't it be said that church committees which did little more than authorize the keeping of such holy artwork on display, such holy statues, whatever might have been fashioned by the creativity of any man or woman, were suggesting that the outer appearance was *evidence* of inner spirituality, and worshippers needn't look any further to be assured that they were in the right place?

The specious nature of all this is apparent. To the question, "Should the Michelangelo who created some of the greatest artwork in the history of mankind be condemned because he *happened* to be homosexual?" Satan would have naive men and women answer with a resounding *no*.

But the truth is otherwise, and none know that better, none know that more intimately than those of us accustomed to feasting on the weaknesses in human character, exploiting these and, thereby, entrapping the unwary.

It is *so* clever!

By accepting the *artists*, whoever they are, as well as the art, the bridge is built, in decades or centuries to follow, for tacit acceptance of his sin, saying in effect if he can do such master-pieces that bring joy to millions, let's just overlook his one *little* problem.

The same holds true for great composers. Peter Ilich Tchaikovsky continues to thrill classical music aficionados. Ask the average ones about his homosexuality, and they would say, "How does that *matter*? It's his music that I adore."

But it does. It does. And it is a matter of which Satan has taken great advantage over the past decade or so, making people wonder if homosexuality can be so bad, so evil, so perverse if a Truman Capote was capable of turning out masterpieces of literature. And in any event, they argue, what he did behind his own bedroom door shouldn't matter to the rest of the popu-lace.

And then came AIDS.

A major defeat for my master, a defeat that tore gaping holes into his very best seductive reasoning.

And yet he bounced back, getting people, lemming-like, to still accept the premise of civil rights for homosexuals rather than imprison them all and throw away the key, as God would do once each gay person died, and was turned over to my master.

A very large percentage of the gay population *enjoy* having pain inflicted upon them, whether by whips, whether by chains, whether by hot wax on their flesh. Immersed in his own perversity, Satan can guarantee that they will get pain beyond their wildest fantasies—but they will not *savor* a single second of it as they scream in agony for all of eternity.

Evil, sinful men redeemed by their special talents, by their refined tastes, by periodic acts of kindness unconnected with the crimes for which they are responsible?

Satan would fool people into saying yes, yes, *yes*!

But take another example:

Hermann Goering, one of the top three Nazis serving Adolf Hitler, enjoyed collecting fine art, antiques—a laudable hobby. Should he be less condemned because of this one aspect of his personality? Hitler himself loved animals, often treated women with great chivalry. Was he somehow less repugnant due to any of this? If Himmler showed kindness to a handful of Jews simply because he liked them, did that mitigate *in the slightest* the horrible treatment he sanctioned against millions of others?

If a fine artist, if an artist of noble output, if any such artist is painting God, painting Jesus Christ, painting the most uplifting scenes from the Bible, and doing so out of divine impulse, gathering up the creativity required from the very center of his being, as a form of his own worship, and to the honor, the glory of the Subject, then that does say something, that does suggest my master has lost the battle with such a man.

But if this artist, Michaelangelo or any of the others, were creating his masterpieces simply for the beauty of the art itself, simply to test his mastery of color and stroke and design, then where is the salvation in that, however impressed may be the admirers who stand and look in awed silence?

It is hard to think in such terms. It is hard to do so in the *real* world. Do human beings withhold their appreciation of a stirring ballad sung by a fine vocalist until they find out about every sin in his life, to see if that appreciation can be legitimatized? Do they refuse help from a doctor until they put him through some kind of quiz to make sure that he passes muster?

Of course not.

But—and this is the issue, is it not?—should they take the ballad, do they take the help from that doctor *as evidence or hint of sanctification?*

Again, of course not.

Yet that is the deception Satan will use to entrap the undiscerning. He will hide the bad with a mask of good. He will say, "What you see is the true self. There is no other. Don't believe the religious hypocrites."

I know.

All too well.

*D*eception.

And nowhere more emphatically than within the Body of Christ.

The little men on television speak of their corrupt doctrines. They rant on about Christians being every bit an incarnation of divinity as was Jesus Christ. They play with their heresies with the fervor of curious children masturbating for the first time, and yet these are old pros doing it in front of millions, an altogether different sort of indecent exposure.

Not only do they build a house on sand, but they build a house that has nothing in its materials to retard the flames that will ignite and consume its very structure.

Soon, I think, *soon that house will be brought down at your feet while you weep over the ashes that are the remnants of your pretensions.*

I know of a large-scale, awful plan of Satan's, a plan to attack the very nerve center of much of the modern Christian world. I can still recall his chuckles of anticipation.

Prime-time news coverage is guaranteed.

It is true, in the human world, as well as in the demonic, that people *do* get what they deserve.

And never more so than with the odious gang of my master's puppets who seem so righteous and caring as they reach out through the airways to take the faith of the elderly, the young, the gullible, and twist it all into a common dagger that my master throws back into the heart of all that is holy and good and decent and honest.

That moment, that moment of paroxysmal fury when the concrete-and-steel-and-crystal empires of the dishonorable majority of those electronic religion sellers, emitting the stench of their spiritual putrescence, become exposed for what they are, propped up movie sets, with no substance whatever, held together only by the dollars that are thrown at their dung-encrusted feet . . . that moment, yes, it is coming, it is roaring in from the north, it surely is, if demonic plans are not thwarted, timed to occur as a crippling blow just before that final, foretold apocalypse in which God will try—oh, how He will try—to scourge the earth of our influence.

For those caught up in the industry of Christianity hoopla, the publicity machinations, it will seem at the start a moment, a time, an event of rejoicing, steeped in self-congratulating speeches, as the powerful and the famous from Christendom gather, majoring as they do in the exteriors, parading their modern white sepulcres, and in this sham, seeming so dedicated, so righteous, while full of the picked-clean bones of those they continue to betray with promises of easy salvation, easy healing, easy money—the event of their assembling together all aglow with spotlights and neon signs and tinselly cheer.

Yet, in the end, the celebrating will not come from any within the Body of Christ—no, it is not this of which I speak but, instead, the collective infernal rejoicing by thousands upon thousands of hovering banshees, my comrades one and all, emerging from Hell to howl their delight at the stinking parade of blind shame that soon would be broadcast from the ashes of itself to the world around, even as that world begins the short ride to Armageddon.

*B*ut for the moment, there is a delay, a wait, which is almost unendurable for the impatient among us....

My master is not an environmentalist. Nor a sentimentalist.

He is uninterested in having a healthy world, a world of beauty.

Scarred landscapes are his children.

Toxic wastes excite him.

Air pollution is an elixir.

Oil spills are accolades.

Ozone depletion he celebrates.

Rivers clogged with fish dead of seeping chemicals fill his days with laughter.

Birds suffocating.

People dying from lungs of rampant cancer.

The eyes of others milky white, sightless because of addictives, whatever else.

Children, thin and pale, leukemia killing them.

Flies on dung and urine and phlegm from lack of sewerage.

Lifeless bodies, stomachs bloated, flesh decaying under the hot desert sun.

Always in the air an odor, the odor that only death brings.

And he stands there, this master of my kind and me, he stands there in the midst of his domain, gloating as ever, while we sing the *alleluias* that have been commanded from times of darkness immemorial, *alleluias* that are his and his alone.

I am very tired," says A'Ful.

"I can understand that," I respond.

"He has me doing the most terrible of deeds."

"And he has me recording them."

"In his eyes they are glorious; in mine they are filth." He launches into recollection then, moments of ignominy, though even that word seems insufficient to describe what my comrade has been forced to do.

AIDS.

He helped to cause the epidemic by planting the seeds of perverse behavior, behavior that obviously violated the laws of God and biology, which are, after all, one and the same.

"The very thought of what gays do among themselves sickens me," he says. "And the knowledge that I was an instigator, that I put before them what the master did with Adam and Eve—promises, Observer, promises of pleasure, promises that God was somehow impotent and, ultimately, the truth of the matter was that they didn't have to worry about

Him at all, that they could go their own way without fear of retribution."

    . . . the convertibles drive by, the flatbed trucks, the people walking in the middle of the street. Some seem, on the surface, quite happy, their faces painted brightly. Quite a number are lifting small bottles to their nostrils and drawing in deep breaths. Others are smoking what is obviously marijuana. A few are dressed in nothing but essentially the lower part of their underwear. There is an abandonment of inhibitions that they embellish with their garish look. Several are kissing not so much out of passion but as a pose for the TV cameras in evidence and, frankly, to shock those not accustomed to things of darkness being played out in the light.*

A'Ful is trembling, his wings drooping behind him.

"The next step was to shift gays from the shame that originally accompanied their behavior to pride, to militant pride that would become, to them, a cause, with lawyers hired to protect their rights, with the media by-and-large geared to brainwash people into thinking that they had any right to have *any* rights at all, that they should be treated in any way like *normal* people."

He laughs cynically.

"Look at the Andy Rooney case," he points out. "All he did was state the truth about these degenerates. All he did was be honest. And he was punished for his words. As soon as he opened his mouth, they were on him."

"Yes," I agree. "You have convinced so many people that to speak out against them is to be guilty of bigotry."

"A master stroke!" A'Ful says with half-hearted jubilation. "Satan applauded me. I should be exaltant."

But it is obvious that he isn't.

The demon responsible is the demon burdened by the significance of what he has done.

"You know, I can hardly wait for Satan to win the war," he adds. "Then I won't have to tolerate these obscene monstrosities any longer."

With that, A'Ful has touched upon an aspect of our master's personality that no mortal journalist, no theologian, no one on the human side has ever stumbled upon, and it can only be that they simply don't know the truth.

Satan has no sense of loyalty, except to those of us who followed him from Heaven, and none can be completely certain about that, though we base our future upon it.

As far as the master is concerned, human beings are absurdly weak puppets whom he can manipulate at will. Once he has emerged victorious, once he has wrested Heaven away from God, he will then turn on everyone who has ever supported him over the many centuries of time. A being with no loyalty, no fidelity, has no compunctions about devastating the ones who helped him to victory—rather like the man who wants to be king and then once he is crowned, disposes of anyone who could be a threat to him, even those who helped him to sit on the throne.

I know. Because I have heard him tell us so.

"They think they do right by doing wrong," he once bellowed. "The pornographers, the drug dealers, the gay libbers—so smart are they? What they don't realize is that I am as appalled by their practices as God is. Nowhere is it written that I look at certain acts in any manner that is different from His own. I find these as repellant as He does."

The impact of that was heavy.

What we do, we do not because any of it is honest or moral or holy. Satan knows what is honest and moral and holy *better than any human being in all of history!* Of all the angels, he was the closest to God, the most magnificent of any of us. Could it *ever* be supposed that none of the divine truths would sink in? Nay, he absorbed into his very being all that God had told us while we yet remained. He saw the beauty of God's plans for the soon-to-be created Human Race. He saw the soaring majesty of what Planet Earth was to be like, free of disease, death, guilt, shame, indeed of anything which would hamper the potential that mankind would be capable of as time passed.

But Satan was willing—and is still willing—to throw all of this away and pervert the truth and deceive the unwary. If there were no knowledge of the truth, then there would be no conception of what he had to subvert in order to gain the victory he sought.

"I *know* that abortion is evil," he went on. "But I am willing to *use* it to tear at the fabric of a supposedly Christian nation—or any other, for that matter. I *know* that there is no such creature—and that is exactly what they are, dumb, brute beasts giving in to their brute passions—I know there is no such creature as an honest, decent, practicing homosexual who deserves even a modicum of respect, but I am willing to fill them up with ego, willing to get them to flaunt themselves in their annual parades *because they are a cancer, like abortion, that will drain away the decent moorings of any society, any civilization that tolerates, yea, that encourages them!*"

He went on and on telling us the sweeping story of what the future would be if we all did what we must to win the war against God.

And then the most stunning revelation of the lot, kept from us until then.

"The human beings we corrupt," he said, "those who pledge allegiance to *me* often do so because they have chosen *me* as the victor. The odds, they say, are in *my* favor. And they assume I will reward them for that choice."

Satan was overcome with laughter, and had to stop talking briefly in order to gain control of himself.

"Yes, I *will* reward them," he said. "I will give them exactly what they deserve."

He paused, surveying the group of demonkind. We all wondered what he would say next.

None of us was prepared.

"I will punish them for their deeds in *precisely* the same manner as promised by God Himself. They *will* roast forever in the lake of fire. The difference is that all of *us* will be watching from a safe distance!"

There it was, the ultimate treachery from the Arch Deceiver, the Prince of Lies!

Countless millions falling over themselves as the centuries passed, falling over themselves in blind obedience to their demonic king, and doing so with one transcendent motivation: that they could indulge their vile pursuits and escape punishment for these as Satan rendered God a foe made powerless by defeat in the eternal warfare between them.

And yet they would heap upon themselves the same eternal goals of fire that God had said *He* would mete out for their sin.

Satan clearly anticipated the moment of seeing so many who once had fallen before him in adulation now thrown into the lake of fire, screaming, "You betrayed us! You betrayed us!"—and the master yelling back at them, "Of course, my foolish ones! If I could betray *Jehovah,* the Creator of all of us, I should hesitate to do the same with *you?*"

But there was more, further indication of how much Satan was motivated by sheer revenge. He planned to take all surviving Christians and force them to engage in the very acts that had seemed so repugnant to them while there was still the expectation that God would win the war.

"How many will cling to their emasculated Creator when they have to have sex with animals?" he said, licking his lips. "They will *beg* me for mercy."

He paused, looking out over his audience, then: *"And I will give them not one drop of that mercy which they will be craving so desperately!"*

*I*s my master the instigator of *all* evil on the face of the planet? Or is he sometimes merely a bystander, gloating over certain events but not directly responsible for these?

He has sought to give the impression that the answer to the first question is yes, and to the second, *never*!

But, of course, he is a liar, and there is little truth in any of this.

Human nature, since the Fall, has been quite capable of mischief, and considerably more, all on its own. In some instances, Satan has had to do no more than provide a mere spark to the ammunition that would have exploded otherwise.

I never realized this more vividly than when I used a mass killer as one of my hosts. I was inside his mind, his soul. I witnessed many of the murders through the eyes of the man responsible, if he could be called a man by any stretch of the imagination—more like a demon wrapped in human flesh, only the thinnest of façades.

But there was one in particular, the grisliest of all. He raped a teenage girl, then cut her into little pieces, then mailed these parts to the editors of the biggest newspapers in the nation.

And sat back, in his then-anonymity, laughing.

Satan chortles at such things. But I don't. I don't at all. I never did. I tolerated my master's perversity as part of the package, so to speak.

. . . *laughing.*

Others died at this killer's hand, mostly teenage girls. In different sections of the country, north, south, east, and west.

He would use disguises, sometimes a moustache and horn-rimmed glasses, sometimes a blonde wig, sometimes shaving all the hair off his head, sometimes—

Always it was night-time when he hit the streets, looking for victims. The young girls responded to him because he was quite handsome. None ever escaped, except the very last. She was the one who helped the police track him down. He was in a warehouse when they trapped him. One of the officers had to be pulled off him as he exploded in anger at someone so evil that he could be responsible for the deaths of nearly forty innocent girls.

I left him long before his execution. Seldom was I more relieved. Countless times I have been *evicted* because of a host's conversion, and it has not especially bothered me, since that is one of the rules of the game, so to speak. And having played the game for a very long time, I have become accustomed to the rules. Usually I have left as a result of the death of my host, cold flesh not a hospitable place, nor helpful to the writing of my book—obviously.

And conversion to Christ was once again the cause. But this time it was not so much that I was kicked out but *liberated,* freed from the shell that had housed me through the most vile of acts, acts so debased that even I find it difficult to contemplate them, to see in memory what he did with the bodies of the innocent after he had committed their murder. I left this host gladly because I couldn't stand the thought that, now he was born again, as they say, he would avoid punishment, that he would be walking the streets of Heaven, while some of his victims who perhaps died without Christ in their lives would be consigned to Hell where my master could torment *them!*

Where was the justice in that? The love?

I remained there, in his death row prison cell as he said those words of acceptance, tears streaming down his face, tears of cleansing and release of all the sin, the anger, the pain that had been bottled up inside him. And in that instant as he died, I was forced to see the utter joy on his face. Yet turning slightly, I watched as the parents of some of the victims showed the anguish that they felt, anguish only partially relieved by the death of the man responsible.

"Can anyone suppose that *this* would do it for us?" a mother said afterwards. "That sending lethal charges of electricity through *his* body would somehow make the future any less empty?"

How *could* I bear the peace on his face after the Holy Spirit entered that despicable soul of his?

I forsook my journal, leaving where it had dropped in that scene of his capture and went off by myself, trying hard indeed to stay away but I could not. I had to return. Then the switch was thrown, and he died.

Outside, there was a celebration. Hot dogs were being sold. And hamburgers. Some folks were munching on heavily-buttered popcorn.

A banner waved in the breeze. "THIS IS FRY-DAY FOR YOU, KILLER!"

They were laughing. The media was there.

A man was playing a guitar.

A celebration I said. A celebration I mean. A grand and glorious event for them.

"This was too good for him," a man, holding a can of beer, said between belches. "He should've been sliced and diced like he did to some of his victims."

He shook the can.

Empty.

"'Vengeance is mine saith the Lord,'" he went on. "I don't buy that crap, you know. It's nothing but a pile of—"

A buddy came up to him, holding out the next can of beer.

"I'm gonna get sizzled tonight," he bragged. "They're gonna have to carry me out."

Beyond the barbed wire fence a hearse had pulled up to the back entrance of the prison.

They all turned and watched.

"Good riddance!"

"Hope you roast in Hell!"

"Hope? Whadda you mean? Where else would that monster be?"

"Thank God he's gone, wherever that is."

A single figure dressed in black stood near the prison as the hearse drove away. Her head was bowed, a veil over her face. Crying, she was.

"Look!" someone shouted. "Look at that broad!"

"Yeh. Acting like she's upset. Man, would I love to get my hands on her. Teach her what's what! Teach her *good*!"

Laughter, raucous, punctuated with blasphemies.

Hey, throw another shrimp on the barbie, will ya?

*I*t is said that the most significant cause of killers such as that one is the kind of abuse-filled childhood from which so many evolve. Uncaring parents strip away their self-respect. And they lash out in anger.

But not all children who are subjected to monstruous suffering in their own homes become mass murderers. Some merely spent the rest of their lives paying another price for the sins of their so-called loved ones.

In this regard, then, some of the more recent cases of child abuse stand out in memory; others, while tragic, fade. (When you have been in on this sort of thing for centuries, a few are bound to rise to the top of your mind while the others are drawn down into the quicksand of your guilt, submerged perhaps permanently, perhaps not.)

But one in particular, indeed, yes. . . .

The burned child.

Not Rothenberg. Not him at all. He is not a candidate for damnation because he accepted Christ as Savior and Lord.

Another.

A child whose father poured gasoline over him and set him on fire.

A child who is scarred for the rest of his life, in mind as well as body.

A child who is, in the eyes of some, a freak.

It happened five years before.

But still the operations are necessary, still pockets of skin puff up, especially on humid days, as body fluids seep in, like air in a balloon. A scalpel must lance these areas so that the poisons can be dabbed out and then new skin taken from other, less-affected parts of the body, and—

In the course of his lifetime, this boy-later-adult-man will have nearly a hundred operations. The costs will reach into the hundreds of thousands of dollars.

He will never marry.

The father has been released from prison.

No community of moral, caring people wants him.

He must be forced down the throats of protesting citizens somewhere.

When he gets settled in, finally, he looks at himself in the mirror, runs fingers over his smooth face, and wonders if his son will ever forgive him.

The son must live not only with his ruined forehead, his cheeks, his chin, the rest of his upper torso, and fingers that will never be fully re-sensitized to touch—he must live not only with this, but with a lingering bitterness, a bitterness that twists his soul, affecting his every relationship.

"I can never be a father," he cries in moments of unquenchable despair, "because no one will ever want to hold me, no one will ever want to kiss me."

A quarter of a century after the burning, he dies, alone, in a room beside a round table with a phone on top and no calls to make.

The flames surround him, their heat licking at every inch of him. He can see a familiar form through the reddish glow, like a phantom.

"Why did you do this to me, father?" the no-longer-boy screams.

His father does not respond, lost in his own anguish.

"You made me so bitter, so filled with hatred that I turned away, from people, from God. I rejected them all, father."

The man does not answer. He cannot. There are no more words because he knows what he has done, and he knows what he must face, and he knows that it will never, never end.

"God damn you!" the no-longer-boy shouted. "God damn you to Hell!"

And then he stops. His pain is transcendent. He has only strength left to cry, as the other is crying, the torment they feel rising in their echoing sobs from that flaming pit throughout eternity.

Your actions damned you both, I add in this my book, recalling his profane words, words I myself hate even though I am still a demon.

You rejected the son, the Son.

I wrote of shed blood some while back, didn't I? Christ shed His blood for redemption; I have shed the blood of others for damnation. In that lies the difference between Him as the master of the saved and Satan as the master of the lost.

But, you know, the Arch Deceiver himself is often the victim of deception.

"*I* put Him there," he will say gloatingly. "I drove men to doubt, then anger, then murder. He died because of *me*!"

I think of that in idle moments when I am not occupying a host or when that host is asleep. I think of how true it must seem to Lucifer. He oppressed Pilate with cowardice; he instilled fear and envy into Caiphas and others, this made easier by their stultiloquent legalism; it was satanic oppression directed against Peter's sin nature that caused the fisherman to deny his Lord three times whereas, earlier, he protested that never would such a thing happen!

It was my master in Judas that—

No, I cannot pass the blame entirely to Lucifer.

Judas was also *my* host. I, too, was indwelling him. And I, I alone, was the one using him to continue my journal.

How much of *me* did he manifest?

How much like bloated, festering, cankered Satan did Judas become?

If I were not the cause, then I had to be the conduit.

It is a truth that has occurred to me before, but each time I have been successful in pushing it aside, in burying it in some outer corner—

(And how like man I am in that regard, how like man indeed, dealing with the truth by frequently pretending that it doesn't exist, that I can escape its implications.)

. . . as I, too, looked up into that tormented face, seeing the trickles of blood from under the thorny crown, hearing the groans of pain as the body twitched and shook and wrenched in final agony, even so words of exquisite supplication escaping softly and with infinite tenderness past those pale and twisted lips, a supplication not rooted in condemnation, not seeking the damnation of those responsible but rather a supplication begging God to forgive the architects of this infamy, and then that final gasp, a small sound really, hardly audible, lasting only for an instant, that final acknowledgement signifying it was finished for Him, it was indeed over.

Truth nailed to bare wooden beams and raised up to be scorned by the multitudes.

And there I was, with the rest of them!

This moment came for me after Judas hanged himself, my journal at his feet, found by a passer-by and taken . . . and I go on, with the next one who will find it, a whore-demon attaching myself to any and all.

Do I have no shame?

Mister, want company for the evening, for the rest of your life?

*W*hat we dignify with the name of peace is merely a short truce, in accordance with which the weaker party renounces his claims, whether just or unjust, until such time as he can find an opportunity of asserting them with the sword.

That, really, is the state of affairs between governments on Planet Earth. Any recent naive talk of peace must be viewed in the light of my master's designs for this battered globe.

Satan is flexible, you see.

He can achieve a great deal in war as well as in peace. In war, the barbaric side of man's nature is ascendent. Atrocities are committed that would have been unthinkable otherwise. The slaughter of hundreds or thousands in a single battle is routine. But then there are the casualties of a score of children in a schoolyard when a nation is at so-called peace.

But peace can also provide a cornucopia of malevolence in other ways for the Prince of Darkness. It is in peace that governments grow lax. It is in peace that morality suffers the seductive doctrines disseminated by my kind through those men and women we succeed in dominating: materialism, dealt a crippling blow by the sacrifices mandated in wartime, rises from its dormant state to ravage the countryside, as it were, a malignant force interpolating itself into the lives of those who stand before its altars in dumb worship.

Peace can turn the minds of men from basic survival to reeking self-indulgence. They grow fat with excess, burdened by the lack of exterior menace; the longer there is peace, the more people are duped into thinking that that is how things always will be.

There is no better example of this than the aftermath of World War I, the "war to end all wars," as peace spread over the world, the possibility of hostilities on that scale just twenty odd years later viewed as only the delusion of irascible cynics or pessimists.

And there is the other consideration: What is peace to some is a slow and excruciating poison to others! Was the state of peace to the Germans peace at all? Or rather a two-decades-long humiliation that went beyond mere shattered nationalistic pride, until the survival of Germany itself seemed very much hanging by a few tattered economic and political threads?

It was at this point the Arch Deceiver introduced the human devil, Adolf Hitler. If King David was a man after God's own heart, then Hitler was a man after the awful depths of Lucifer's twisted and malignant self. My master was the *Fuehrer's* master perhaps more completely than with any of the demonkind, if that could be considered possible. Satan remade Hitler's personality into his own image.

When the extermination camps were built, Satan merely constructed his own version of Hell through his human puppets, telling millions of people that if they weren't Aryans or they didn't give *him* complete obedience, they would be tormented unto death. When that death did overwhelm them, Satan was given yet another opportunity with the unredeemed ones to pile on more anguish, this time in the *real* Hell.

*O*nce there was such a fear of communism. Now the resurgence of National Socialism is cause for increasing panic.

How Satan rubs his gnarled hands together at the thought of *that*!

He has the elements in place, through various groups such as the Ku Klux Klan, the Aryan Front movement headed by a chap in southern California who is as scary underneath as he seems nice on the surface.

"He's ripe for us," Satan only recently told us. "He hates niggers, he hates kikes, spicks, he—"

On and on Satan ranted, enjoying the sounds of those hateful labels, enjoying the prospect of fomenting a new civil war within the United States, but on a much wider scale than that of a century and a half ago.

"The harvest is at hand," he proclaimed.

An army of disaffected young people.

The runaways. The abused. Seething with anger, hungry for revenge.

"And I shall give them the guns to blow the brains out of the generation that has been tormenting them," Satan told us.

At the same time he has been pushing, pushing, pushing the mothers and the fathers who are now the objects of their contempt, inculcating that generation with the doctrine of disposable parenthood: If you don't want a child, abort the thing; if you don't want the continued responsibility of the offspring that do survive this modern holocaust, then kick the creature out of the house, and get on with your own life.

By the thousands. Pouring out into the streets. By the hundreds of thousands. Clogging the arteries of this present society. Looking for a way to get even.

And so they band together in angry, seething groups to fuel each others' fire, groups which provide exactly what they are seeking.

Hate fears above all to be delivered of itself.

I cannot remember where I read those words or by whom they were written. But they are true, you know. For some, hatred is the alpha and the omega of all that they are. And it must continue, this corrosive venom that seems almost to replace blood and marrow. Once the original object is overwhelmed, defeated, cast aside as impotent, there must be another, and the process is endless, for were it not, were all the objects of all the prejudice, the bigotry, the lust for vengeance gone, sucked up and spit out, then that hatred would turn unimpeded upon itself and—

I have seen such as are possessed in this manner. I have seen them in every age of history. I have used many as my hosts.

And I serve one.

Yes, I do.

Oh, God, I do.

*T*here are many plans in which my master is involved.
Most are set to spring into action at the same time,
each a piece in the puzzle of his design for the collapse of
civilization, and his consequent takeover.
Especially interesting is the one he is working out with those the
world no longer fears.

Especially indeed.

A dozen men sitting in chairs around a table in a room bare of any other furniture. Their expressions are intense. Faintly, in the background, there are the sounds of a military band.

"It is time that we . . . we . . . what is that American expression?" one of them, tall, thin, owlish-looking, says.

"Pull the plug?" another offers.

"Yes, pull the plug!" Owl says. "He has gone further than we thought. He has gotten carried away with his reforms."

"We are at a dangerous crossroads," a huge man responds, his frame that of a grizzly bear. "If he is allowed to go on, the survival of communism is at stake."

"He must be stopped, we all agree, is that not so?" Owl asks of the gathering.

They all answer in the affirmative.

"The day the Libyans posing as Iranians and armed by the Iraqis blow up that . . . that . . . ," Bear adds, not quite sure of the target, but sure that there is a target.

Someone reminds him.

"Yes! That is the one. As soon as that happens, there will be a worldwide reaction. Tell me, do they have everything they need?"

"They do," Owl replies. "Forged passports. A cache of explosives near a place in America called Colorado Springs."

"Gardens of the Gods," Bear adds.

"Quite safe?"

"Completely."

They adjourn in a few minutes, but Owl and Bear remain behind.

"It is an exquisite bit of planning," Owl acknowledges.

"Truly it is," Bear agrees. "In the midst of the chaos, with Reformer siding with the Americans and reacting in anger against the terrorists, we leak a story that there is an invasion of Iran being concocted, with Reformer pledging the resources of our vast spy network to help and, we intimate, perhaps much more than that."

Bear paused, sipping for a few seconds on a glass of vodka.

"We have an agent of ours from the PLO go in and assassinate him," he adds, "blaming it again on the Iranians."

"Suddenly the world turns against Iran more than ever before," Owl says, gleaming, "plunging it into its greatest isolation of the post-shah period."

"Then one of our own men takes over in the vacuum left by Reformer's death, and, posing as their true friends, we form a secret alliance with the Iranians, supplying them with arms."

"Will China go along?" Owl asks. "Can we be sure of that?"

"We can be sure," Bear says ominously. "The blueprint has already been drawn up. Beijing is satisfied."

Reformer had changed since 1985. Once a through-and-through communist, he seems to have very nearly abandoned the Party's decades-long goals.

"But the Party has abandoned the goals of Lenin and Marx," he remarked at one point.

What was the turning point for this man?

There were two.

One, the Leningrad earthquake.

Two, the Petrinsky nuclear disaster.

Reformer saw the depth of human suffering arising from both. His people, his fellow Russians had died by the tens of thousands.

He stood in the midst of the quake-shattered buildings, heard the cries of the dying, the injured.

And felt utterly helpless.

"We just do not have the capabilities enjoyed by the Americans," he whispered. "We learned little about disaster response, because we had had little experience in that regard. It was the western world that had their earthquakes, their tornadoes. We had been through our blizzards but little else."

"And nuclear plant safeguards, sir," the aide pointed.

"Yes," Reformer agreed. "Nothing tragic would happen to us, of course—only to the Americans, with or without our sabotage."

In the case of Petrinsky, he could look only from a distance, the region completely unsafe for any on-the-spot tour.

"The deaths, at this point, will go over a hundred thousand," an aide told him, "possibly much greater."

He gasped at the news.

"But there is more, sir," the aide added. "Many will take years to die! For some, it will cause leukemia; for others, lymph cancer. Brain tumors will be another source of suffering and death. Also, leprosy may be involved, sir."

"Oh, God . . . " he said, his voice choking.

"God, sir?"

He waved his hand impatiently through the air.

"Go on," he said. "Are there more details?"

"The information I have given you concerns only the generations that have been born. There are pregnant women who will give birth to monstrosities, pathetic little human-creatures with misplaced eyes, with. . . ."

The aide stopped for a moment, his eyes moist, a sudden headache throbbing at his temple.

"Children who will face retardation," he went on with visible effort, "and unknowable numbers who may not have purely physical disabilities, at least like the others, but will experience emotional and related problems because their metabolism has been dealt a wrenching and devastating blow."

The aide could not go on, his mind filled with the details of a number of reports that he had compiled for presentation to the general secretary.

There was silence for a moment.

"We were so concerned about conquering country after country, about expanding the Soviet sphere of domination that we let our motherland go to hell," Reformer said.

"Do you mean that literally, sir?" the aide interjected.

Reformer only looked at him without answering.

*T*he blueprint. . . .

They think themselves so clever and to a degree, they are, in human terms, devilishly clever. They allowed Reformer to ascend to a position of power, offering only token resistance to his plans for reform. All the while, they sat back while he seemed to be amassing more and more power. He was *their* man; they *wanted* him to be in command.

Past tense.

He is not now the same man he was as at the beginning.

No, he is no longer one of *them!* Rather, he is their diametric opposite, with some streaks of good, some pockets of decency, though trapped by a lifetime of atheistic dogma. Perhaps Reformer would like it to be different, but that cannot be, at least not in any reasonable scenario that can be conjured up; yet unlike us demons, he is *capable* of making an attempt to change the scheme of things, of letting some acts of noble intent break through the nihilism. Accordingly, prepared for the worst conceivable eventuality, his opponents—termites in the house he is building, eating away at the structure—are readying themselves for that moment when it will collapse and they will reassume command.

But in the meantime. . . .

Ah, yes, that is the brilliance of the scheme—they think it theirs but, of course, they are nothing more than the recepticles of it. In the meantime, NATO has been greatly altered; the two Germanies have been integrated, the communists able at last to gain positions in the new *Western* government, which was otherwise an impossibility, even though they may use the convenient label of socialists—indeed, how easily mere labels fool the gullible.

What a difference a year made back then!

You do not lock your doors to those who are no longer your enemies.

You open your house and welcome them.

The communists no longer need to use force to break in; they are being given the key.

All things work together for evil to those who are in slavery to Satan.

Sounds familiar, doesn't it?

*B*ut that plot isn't the only one by unholy men in secrecy planning events of death and destruction. Another is being executed step-by-step from Germany. Though half a century has passed since the Holocaust, for some Germans, it seems like only yesterday.

The industrialists.

Behind reunification is a hidden agenda. The sons of the same men whose profits benefited from the use of cheap Jewish labor at concentration camps built near German factories—I know this was not at all a coincidence because one of my hosts was a vice-president of Siemans AG and I heard a great deal about men with big companies who helped the Nazis pay for the costs of erecting the camps with the condition that the locations be in close proximity to certain factories whenever possible or, when this couldn't be achieved, that train-loads of Jews be taken wherever the industrialists desired at any given moment—these sons still with billions of dollars at their disposal are supporting the neo-Nazi movement world-wide, but with particular emphasis in the United States.

Famous companies continue with remnants of the old mindset, directors and major stockholders and others who skim off part of their earnings to pay for the expansion of the Aryan skinhead movement, causing the deaths of Jews, blacks and Catholics, sending bombs to mayors, senators and anyone else who may be standing in their way.

I remember coming across a book by an author whose credits included a notable history of the Third Reich. A German himself, he lamented over his countrymen's historic tendency toward tyranny, toward violence, toward the destruction of any who disagree with them.

Adolf Hitler was one German who rose to the top of this garbage heap. But, even as I think the thought, I realize that there are a hundred like him yet entrenched in that land, a hundred or more who, given the opportunity, would create a thousand new Dachaus, Auschwitzes, Treblinkas, Mauthausens and others.

A few years ago, one of my hosts stayed at a mountainside motel in Colorado. Food eaten in the adjoining restaurant turned out to be quite bad. My host was afflicted with stomach cramps so severe that he thought he was going to die. He called the front desk for medicine, and was told that there was none, that he would have to drive to a community seven miles away at midnight, and hope that a store would still be open. My host begged for help but the assistant manager remained unsympathetic. My host then accused the man of acting like a Nazi. The reply was unforgettable: "I *am* a Nazi. Did you ever think that Hitler might have done the world a favor by getting rid of six million Jews?"

The Oregon courtroom that saw a judgment of millions of dollars against Tom Metzger, the force behind the growth of the American skinhead movement, also saw him declare that people like him were in government and industry all across the United States. "We are everywhere," he said proudly.

We are everywhere. . . .

America has those in secret places planning terror campaigns that have no connection with Middle Eastern terrorists
but which will cause havoc all their own.

And the money, yes, the money for all of this, the money
for the weapons and so much else, that money comes from
wood-panelled offices in Hamburg and Frankfurt and all across
Germany.

Some Germans haven't changed, you see. I know. I know
all of it. I know the irony of what is happening—how money
spent by Americans on German cars and cameras and many
other products is being rerouted back into the land of the free
from the land of the swastika.

Why does no one stop this insanity?

Simple. Money that buys weapons also buys people, also
buys silence. And when the money fails, there are the sudden
"heart attacks" from poisons undetectable by even the most
advanced tests.

I know it all, as I have said. I was there at the beginning.

When my master rose up before us and spoke of the good
old days of "burning Jews and hanging niggers."

*B*I cannot say that I *like* being in cemeteries, and yet these places of bone and worms and crypts of the dead do seem like home more often than not; I am, after all, a creature of darkness, of death, of sheer and total damnation. I wear a tattered cloak of sorrow—I speak metaphorically since, as spirit, I wear nothing—a cloak of tears in an eternal night-time of torment, ravaged by fear of coming Armageddon.

Tears. . . .

Many are shed in the cemeteries of my life, yet there is an attempt to put everything in the best light. Look at the good deeds, it will be said. How many poor had the deceased kept from starvation? Surely that counts for something in the kingdom of the Almighty. How many missionaries had he supported? How much—?

Acts aimed at redemption but deprived of that goal in the divine scheme of all creation!

Nothing can be *done*. God did it all. There is but one requirement: simple faith.

But often the messengers get in the way of the message, because those who minister to the thirsty with apparent waters of redemption bring with them instead leather bags of contaminated filth.

I remember a funeral at Forest Lawn. . . .

Major Star had died. His agent was there. His manager. His fans. The media. A dozen limousines. Press vans.

The eulogy was given by pompous, egomaniacal Arch Strutter.

"This man's *deeds* speak for themselves," he said. "He lived his *seed faith* to the fullest. *And God will reward him accordingly!*"

How awful!

There I was, as a demonic intruder unknown to any of them, and I had a firmer grasp of theological reality than that overblown, opportunistic fool.

Yet I thought over Strutter's words, and realized how true they were, though not in the way he intended.

" . . . God will reward him accordingly."

Indeed.

I stayed quite a length of time at that funeral. Others stood up, and spoke about Major Star, his decades in the movie business, all his fans world-wide, the total box-office draw he had exerted.

And then those present went on to the wake-like affair at the studio where Major Star had been under contract. Several individuals became drunk and there was a bit of a brawl.

In corners and at tables, huddled among themselves, they talked of Major Star's vanity, his appalling temper, his disdain for showing any degree of respect for his co-workers.

"What a bum!" declared a man who had earlier stood up and praised Major Star.

"You've really changed your tune," another at that table observed.

"That was good business, good PR. This is reality."

Days later, ads were run in *Daily Variety* and *Hollywood Reporter* heralding Major Star's impact upon the entertainment industry, that there would never be anyone like him ever again.

Behind closed doors, there were sighs of relief all over town.

ot far from Forest Lawn was another cemetery, adjacent to a church dating back to the turn of the century. It hadn't reached landmark status as yet, and was rather run-down. An old woman had just been buried there that same day. Out front was a battered, rusty sedan.

There were only three mourners, not hundreds.

Her daughter, her son-in-law, her granddaughter.

" . . . left behind no worldly goods," the minister was saying, "at least not the tangible kind, not limousines, not mansions, not hundreds of suits and pairs of shoes and millions of dollars in the bank. She left behind only one thing . . . a legacy of love."

His voice broke, for an instant; he coughed, then went on speaking.

"She had no one except her family. She outlived everyone else, all the old friends from decades before. When she died, she was with her family. She made one last comment to them."

. . . the clouds be rolled back.

"That's what she saw, Lord. Let me add one other line from a famous old hymn: 'I'd rather have Jesus than silver or gold; I'd rather be His than have riches untold; I'd rather have Jesus than houses or land.'"

It was soon over, this little ceremony. The daughter, the son-in-law, the granddaughter lingered, then left.

I turned to go.

But I was not alone.

Stedfast. . . .

Stedfast had come, for a moment, to pause at the grave.

"She was radiant, Observer," he said.

"I suppose she was, Stedfast," I replied.

"The lines disappeared, the gray along with it, the arthritis, the dulled mind—all that remained in her coffin, you know."

"You are always right, Stedfast."

This unfallen one turned to me, sorrow in his countenance.

"She went to glory," he said.

"But not me," I said in return.

Stedfast nodded.

"No, not you, my—" he started to say but stopped, doing the spirit-equivalent of biting his lip.

—friend.

That was what he meant. In Heaven we were close . . . we were created together, we worshipped at the Throne together.

Now there was no continuing bond—a broken thing perhaps, something shriveled up, mocking the former oneness, attendant with this the aging memories of salvation thwarted among the multitude of victims over which demons have been rampaging since the beginning of time, the ever-present residue of their torment haunting me in this my world of insubstantiality, ghostly echoes of remembered souls ripped from mortal shells and flung at the feet of my rapacious master, who would scoop them up as he wished when he was personally intent or hand them over to other demons awaiting such when he couldn't be bothered, preferring instead other prey, while they had their way with a new plaything.

"That old woman did but one thing, Observer," Stedfast said then, and nothing further.

Fairest Lord Jesus.

Stedfast did not have to fill in the blanks.

I knew. I had known for a very long time.

A truth encompassing this old woman's destiny, and mine as well. Her choice, the only redemptive one for eternity.

He will I cherish, He will I honor.

Which I never did, which I cannot, which mandated with harsh and compelling justice my entry not in the Book of Life— aglow with the sanctioning verdicts of presiding Divinity—but another . . . of judgment unmitigated, with names from every age, penned in blood spilt on ten thousand times ten thousand battlefields of one sort or another over the centuries of times past . . . not of life transcendent and joyous is it to be with those whose names denote their sad and condemned multitude— nothing, in fact, but the soul-encrusted corridors of Hell itself.

*D*espicable people dressed in expensive suits and backed by piles of money and not a few tactics of intimidation hold sway in the industry that Major Star left behind. Those who were glad that he was no longer on the scene will nevertheless latch onto another puppet put out there by the ever-powerful gangsters who wait in the shadows of the industry.

Many are Italian, or it might be said with greater accuracy—though being accurate never has been my master's strong suit—that they have been seduced away from the decency, the simple and pure human warmth typical of most Italians. The numbers of those thus born have shrunk, this loss of their exclusivity continuing to provoke much dissension within the Mafia, since there has been strong Sicilian pride evidenced in their earlier dominance of the makeup of the various mafioso families. Now, those from this particular region are joined by many awful human swine of the lowest possible sort from other nationalities, demons in fleshly garb, spawning all sorts of indecent things which cause so many innocent ones to be dragged down in the dirt along with them.

They profess to care about the racial bigotry they stir up, hiding behind this ludicruous attempt to legitimatize themselves as they wrap a nation's flag around their behavior—but in fact they are interested only in power, in money, in sex-for-hire, and indeed, as such, they are tremendously effective allies of Satan's, doing his bidding in arcane ways that fatten their pocketbooks as well as their egos. . . .

That funeral for Major Star is only part of the story regarding untold numbers of people in the entertainment world. This industry is such a ripe field for demonic harvest that Satan has periodically toyed with the idea of designating a special section of Hell for agents, producers, movie studio presidents, actors, and so on.

"I shall call it Heartbreak Hotel," he says as he muses over the notion. "Yes! That is a good one."

He laughs at his own joke but he *has* hit the mark.

The top man at one of the major studios uses the power of his position to seduce any attractive young actor who catches his eye.

Never was this more flagrantly apparent than when his studio created a new series about young people, and a strong cast was hired. The lead actor was approached by the studio head and told that if the two did not become lovers, the actor would be dismissed within forty-eight hours. The young man refused. The next morning he received his walking papers, and another actor hired who was more "accommodating."

The original actor's scenes were cut and his replacement refilmed all of these. One problem: The actor who refused to go to bed with the studio head was still listed in *TV Guide* as starring in the series the week it debuted, and there was one quick night scene which somehow escaped being cut; the original actor was seen quite clearly. No explanation was ever offered publicly.

Since then, his replacement has done nicely, with movie roles being offered, and the series itself enjoying a measure of popularity as a high profile draw for younger viewers.

Satan loves it when truths are twisted or lies simply substituted. A great deal of that goes on in Hollywood. It is not difficult to see this in so many of the films that are produced, when immorality is raised up as normal, even laudable—and when filthy personal lives are not only not condemned, but those living such lives become influential in any event.

I once had as a host a rotund actor, one of the perennially popular stars, who had a weakness for teenage boys and young men. He would spend considerable time in a certain restaurant on Sunset Boulevard, eyeing the customers. The owner was paid off handsomely for allowing him to use the restaurant as a kind of jungle in which he stalked his prey.

Then there is that star of a medical series who has had the same male lover for more than twenty years.

The one-time television talk show host who is seldom without his latest male conquest when he goes to various show-business parties.

The supposedly rugged star of a once top-rated western series who is unable to get by without a new lover every few weeks, the AIDS crisis doing little to his sexual appetite.

Others have noted the reality I knew all along, that 60 percent or more of the casting directors are homosexuals or lesbians. Most are incapable of offering an honest evaluation about an actor's talent if they encounter someone whom they find sexually appealing. Step-by-step, an expanding number of young people are drawn into an addictive world of rampant perversion because it is either that they succumb to the "casting couch syndrome" or give up any hope of vibrant careers.

Yet little of this is ever chronicled by an industry that supposedly relishes freedom of expression, and which is more than eager to "expose" the sins of Christians, conservatives, and others who have been criticized over the years. The reason is simple, Satan's success is virtually absolute: Scripts dealing with

gay subject matter or using gay characters are regularly submit-
ted to one or more gay and lesbian media groups for their
approval, only approval is not the word used. The implications
are camouflaged by words such as "consultation" or "out of a
desire to fight bigotry." All very noble-sounding, though nearly
every demon knows the truth and delights in it.

I am a demon, and yet there is no delight that I can feel,
as hard as I try, when I find such a powerful industry as the
television and movie interests controlled by gays or their sym-
pathizers. Satan is delighted, of course. But I am not.

But such sin does not show the full extent of corruption in
Hollywood—a significant part of it, yes, but by no means all.

Bribes are commonplace. Extortion is part of the fabric of
the business, if not by the mobsters, then by the unions—even
those not shackled to the mob, which is only a handful, to be sure.
(It is interesting that organizations supposedly in business to
protect the rights of masses of people end up being corrupted by
handfuls of violent opportunists with ties to big crime bosses.)

Ah, the mob.

This kind of human garbage get their mansions through
the profits made on the backs of the wrecked lives of their
customers. They tool around town in their Mercedes and their
Rolls and their Jaguars, driven by their hired help, smoking their
imported cigars, and not looking beyond their bullet-proof
glass at the devastation left behind.

It is not that being rich is sinful, obviously it isn't. But
becoming rich off of the blood and innocence of others is. And
how clever they are; when anyone calls them evil, calls them filth,
they hide behind the accusation of bigotry—bigotry against their
wealth, bigotry against their nationality, bigotry against their rough
upbringing—waving it like a sword of offended righteousness.

That is their plan!

It is a way of diverting harsh scrutiny from their dirty
businesses. They have *allowed* the stereotypes, the bigoted buzz
words, to gain wide acceptance as a handy tool to make people
feel ashamed of thinking *that* way.

In the meantime, they will continue providing the drugs that the Hollywood crowd craves. They will buy control of an ever-expanding number of businesses, from studios and production companies to catering services and a great many others.

The drugs, yes, but also the prostitution, the gambling, anything that is illicit and from which they can make a profit!

My master has always been convinced that drugs are among his most effective weapons. They are the means by which we can gain access to an individual, and then my kind take over completely.

Satan's pleasure in this regard seems almost orgasmic in its intensity. The pain of the drug addict is something he craves. The more people who become hooked, the happier he is.

"I can weaken any group, any company, any branch of government if I can just get them to try cocaine, to try crack or other drugs," he has said. "These eat away at their will, destroy their self-respect, and leave nothing in return, nothing except an open door for us!"

Satan has a very complete blueprint in terms of drugs. It began with the so-called Woodstock generation. It continues for decades afterward. By the year 2000, he wants drug use to be commonplace among elected officials, whether the mayor of a city, a senator, a cabinet member—one right after the other.

"The more frequent, the less shocked people will be," he tells us periodically. "The first case is scandalous. The second is alarming. But through sheer repetition, by the time it is announced that the hundredth official has been indicted, the public will yawn, the public will count it as yesterday's news."

"Or become so enraged that they mobilize and do something about it," I pointed out on one occasion.

"Perhaps," Satan replied. "But it's worth the gamble, don't you agree?"

I nodded in agreement, my thoughts turning to the addicts, the poor addicts, who had given over their souls so willingly.

As I myself have done.

But corruption in Hollywood cannot be laid wholly at the feet of the drug lords. Human greed isn't a trait peculiar to gangsters.

Much attention was paid to the case of a humorist in his suit against one of the major studios. They stole his script and made millions, yet feigned innocence. Yet this is but one of scores or more piled high like manure in Hollywood, and kept quiet by people not wanting to attack the sources of their livelihood.

I have been in a room with actors as they are being manipulated by mogul-types, lies streaming from the ugly little mouth of the producer or generic studio executive about misappropriated funds. Inevitably, I want to suddenly materialize, and shriek before this smooth-talking swine in my true disgusting form, "We are controlling you. We are in charge of your every thought, word, and deed. *Now get a good look at what your masters are really like!*"

I have watched the brilliant careers of decent men and women plummet because they had the courage to stand up to— even expose—the atrocities of major Hollywood executives.

I have seen these evil ones leave the life of the flesh and enter *our* world, shedding mortality and donning the cape of damnation. Many show remorse; many beg for a second chance. But in the game in which my kind and I are principal players, there is nothing of the sort. Once that old body is gone, there is no opportunity to do it all over again, to improve their chances in "the next life" despite what certain popular actresses keep trying to get those dumber than they are to believe.

Yes, Hollywood continues to be a place of dreams, as it has been for more than half a century.

Before the nightmares take over.

At Heartbreak Hotel.

*T*here is heartbreak at another place but it is not a hotel, though it has many people staying there.

It's called a rest home, but it is also, in a separate building on the same grounds, a sanitarium. For either the old or the mentally ill, and, often, the line is blurred between the two, it is a miserable life that they are called upon to lead.

It is not a place that demons frequent.

Is that surprising?

In earlier periods of history, when mental illness was more or less automatically equated with demonic possession, Satan had a field day, as the expression goes, playing upon the ignorance of the times, ignorance that gave him the credit in cases with which he had no connection or, as in some, no *continuing* connection.

"Those were the days of rich harvest," he would say as he reminisced. "While people became ill because of the pressures they faced, which had nothing to do with our kind, or because of chemical imbalance, or other instigating circumstances, all of *us* could ignore *them*, could rejoice that they descended to the misery we *would* have inflicted, but which didn't cost us a single precious moment. Human nature and human society did our job for us, so we could go on and *really* possess countless others."

"Pushovers, master?" I offered.

"Yes, that *is* the right word, Observer."

"Thank you, master."

But in the final stages of the twentieth century, with so much presumed enlightenment, it would seem that Satan had gone from feast to desperate famine.

Not so.

"There was never anything particularly appealing about possession," he added. "It was a great deal of work in many instances, and when we encountered exorcism, not at all pleasant in the final analysis."

He rubbed his talons together with delight.

"Now we get the same result, and all we have to do is sit back and watch the spectacle! It is even better than during the Dark Ages."

The "spectacle" was obvious in that place of confinement. For the elderly, the afflictions of Alzheimer's and other forms of senility were especially satisfying to Satan. He had never forgotten the cause of all the pain, all the suffering that was visited upon this planet where he has been running rampant for so long.

"If Adam and Eve had never given in," he said, "we would not have had a battle to fight, let alone win or lose. We would have been trapped, Observer, rendered impotent by righteousness all around us. Christ would never have had to die for the redemption of mankind."

He stopped ever so briefly, visions of might-have-been crossing his mind. I shared those with him in that moment, not by reading his thoughts—which I couldn't do—but because, with greater frequency, the truth of what we caused to be destroyed came through to me as well. Still, as with Satan, I rejoiced when I could squelch them, and not have to face the truth yet again, a world without sin, a world in which death never occurred, a world of joy and peace and perfect union with Almighty God.

Not the small parcel of the kind of world I see before me now. Aging men and women shunted aside by offspring who cannot be bothered. Many unable to control their bodily processes, their actions, their hallucinations.

Some may be the way they are through a lifetime of abusing their bodies by pills, by alcohol, by other drugs— legally or otherwise—by promiscuous acts of intercourse with partner after partner. B-y thinking they have escaped punishment in this life only to discover that they have not, they have been reduced to shells of flesh housing souls of torment that do not have to wait until confinement in hell before they taste condemnation.

Others are quite ill, perhaps irreparably so, not particularly as a result of their own sin but in direct connection with the sins of their parents—abuse in childhood robbing them of any dignity, any fulfilment, any joy, anything at all but wallowing in a loathsome pit of sweat and tears and blood and—

How haughty some once had been. The proud and defiant prostitute servicing politicians and millionaires and other "society" clients, now a mumbling hag who shouts obscenities at colorless walls.

The Middle Eastern despot who exhorted millions to a bloody "holy war" and yet lived a life of such unholiness that he rivalled a demon in his behavior, now a pathetic figure indeed being abused by fellow patients.

The hotel magnate, the mayor, the Academy Award-winning actress, now confined, their former worlds shut out.

"The mind," I recall Satan having said, tapping his head as he did so. "If you gain control of even a single human mind, anything is possible."

He had that right, my master did.

If you gain control of even a single human mind. . . .

But little of this *had* to be to the extreme of driving people insane, though such cases did give Satan near-erotic joy. It could stop short, far short, and still be a victory, without the clinically-defined insanity *per se*.

"They're the invisible maniacs-waiting-to-be," he added, "in every village, in every town, in every city and every nation on this planet, Observer."

The streets are filled with ample evidence of the genius of Satan's plan. Only the diagnosed cases are confined to institutions or, rather, the *extreme* ones are. There are millions of men and women and not a few children who are like time bombs ready to explode, the maniacs to whom Satan referred.

"My warriors," Satan had remarked just a short while earlier, then corrected himself. "No, it is more accurate to say that they are my secret agents, the members of my demonic CIA."

There is a conventional wisdom that people who walk, who talk, who smile, who eat, drink, go to the bathroom, have sex, that these people are *functioning*, and, therefore, they are largely okay, and represent no danger to society.

One of Satan's most powerful delusions.

Because in so many instances he is gaining control of that which cannot be *seen* . . . he is gaining control of their minds.

The mass media are culpable, instilling in people desires that may never have existed before or, at least, lain dormant without ever being awakened.

How the master loves those who write their scripts to make adultery seem like *fun!*

"Fun," yes, one of the ugliest words in all of human language: fun to watch dirty movies, fun to get drunk, fun to go on a drug trip, fun to take to bed as many members of either sex as you can, fun to "do it" with children.

"We can destroy multitudes with that one word," Satan sneered more than once.

If it isn't fun, don't do it.

Letting the world have fun is devastating enough, but when fun is able to creep into the church, then Satan becomes personally involved instead of delegating so much to various demons.

Worshipping God is *fun*.

Satan hit hard with that.

Bring on the bands. The celebrity singers. The multi-media events. Compete with television.

Become a fun-filled show!

Advertise. Promote.

I remember one service I attended in a high-school auditorium one Sunday morning. A new ministry had begun there, and it would greatly expand in time, with satellite ministries in a dozen cities around the country.

I did not stay long. I saw that my master had done a brilliant job of infiltrating that group with the "fun" doctrine. No need for me to waste my time there.

The music was fun. The hand-waving, highly-charged emotional atmosphere felt *good*. Feeling good was a tributary of River Fun. Be happy. God wants you with a smile on your face. Give no time to pain, to sorrow. You're in the Lord's Good-Time Place.

In a short while I left the sanitarium. I saw a man slobbering food down his face. I turned away.

Have fun, you all.

I   *t is closer now, that event embodying our impatient fury.*
     It is but a little while, just a little while. . . .
     My present host is an influential executive involved in
     the field of publishing—Christian publishing. Satan
was very pleased that he could be taken over.

"This one is quite promising," he tells me. "We need all the
Trojan horses we can get."

He is a Trojan horse because he is one of ours, yet they think
he is one of theirs. He seems to bring so much that is needed to the
Body of Christ: money, marketing experience, contacts.

"We're going to shake up the entire Christian publishing
community," he tells his staff one day. "We're going to bring a
backward industry right into the twentieth century and beyond."

"But, sir, do you think it's a good idea to be publishing
these New Age books alongside our Christian books?" an
editorial assistant tremulously asks.

"No problem!" he responds. "I plan to buy out an existing
publishing firm, and put all the Christian stuff there. We'll keep the
New Age garbage with the parent company."

"Is New Age philosophy garbage?" another staffer asks.

"New Age or Christian, doesn't matter," the publisher says. "The bottom line—that's what I worship. Anything else *is* you-know-what piled high."

"But everybody will see what is happening, sir," the assistant adds. "What if they figure it out?"

"Look, in time, it won't matter. That crowd gets used to just about anything. I'll give the guys at this Christian house the biggest budget they ever had. They can buy any author they want."

"But some authors aren't for sale," the assistant persists. "I can't picture that guy from Nebraska being up for grabs. Or a lot of others I can think of. That deceased one specializing in the cults certainly wouldn't have been. I can name quite a few authors who continue to stick to their convictions regardless of the money factor."

"However, the ones that *can* be bought lock-stock-and-barrel surely include some of the biggies," the publisher counters. "I remember that guy who had been with a family-owned firm for ten years, then an English publisher waved a lot of bucks in front of him, and his sense of loyalty went into deep freeze overnight."

The assistant lapses into silence.

And so it goes.

How smart, I think amidst the heat without end.

For a long time, the Christian publishing industry seemed almost impregnable. It began as a group of people dedicated to ministry, with books and magazines used as instruments to spread the Great Commission.

And then. . . .

It changed.

It changed so drastically—but not all at once: a questionable book here, a slick Madison Avenue-style marketing plan there, a little sacrifice of ethics from time to time, one Luciferian inroad after another, step-by-step until—

Ah, yes, the very last part of my book.

I think it was that Satan had a sense of the end approaching, of Armageddon around the corner, of the plan involving Soviet communists and militant Muslims coming to fruition. Yet even so, it was true that he had precious few opportunities left. There wasn't a lot more he could do with drugs. Political corruption had been milked for all it was worth. AIDS seemed to have put the homosexual thing on hold, at least for awhile, though there was still some manuevering room here.

"We have to hurry," he said at one point. "I suspect the Rapture will be soon. We have to do more to prepare the way for the Antichrist."

The End Times.

Was that period so close at last? Was it—?

*W*e met often in the closing decade of the twentieth century, discussing that brilliant planned attack again and again, waiting for the right circumstances.

It would involve terrorists, yes, as I have said before, as Satan ultimately decided, and every detail would have to be coordinated flawlessly.

But the right target had to be picked. Blowing up just any church wouldn't do it, although we briefly considered that one with all the glass.

Finally, the ideal target was on the horizon, the attack constituting a blow against the entire Christian communications industry. It had to be one that would leave the most awful devastation in its wake.

And then our allies elsewhere would spring into action, men insatiably jealous over the accomplishments of their leader, men who were instead setting in place their own awfulness, a plan that would synchronize so well within the overall design being hatched by Lucifer the Magnificent.

In the end, my fellow demonkind were the losers, of course, despite our anticipatory illusions of rejoicing. But meanwhile they gave in to the fantasy.

They, I say?

Nay. More than they. . . .

Even me.

Part II

A huge dome.

I stand before its gleaming newness.

Like two very large saucers placed on top of one another, the exterior made entirely of crystal panes laid over large round girders. The afternoon sun reflects off its surface, blindingly at times.

I stand before the monument—and it is every bit that—built to last through more than one century. It has been crafted of the finest building materials: the crystal imported from Italy, the steel especially furnaced for maximum stress, the concrete, mixed by a special team hired to make sure there were no defects, the terra-cotta floors polished to a shine. There were miniature nuclear-powered generators, a state-of-the-art communications system that included ultra-stereo amplifiers-receivers-speakers throughout the main hall, and high-tech gadgets of every variety. A stunning architectural achievement by any yardstick.

Babel.

The building had its detractors from the very beginning, those who questioned the *need*, the *wisdom* of it, cautioning that God could never bless extravagance—whether ostensibly in His honor or not. The tens of millions of dollars it cost could have been halved, at the very least, and the difference used to fund missionaries overseas, erect a few more rescue missions to help the homeless, and still have enough left over to start scholarships for Christian students in virtually every state in the nation.

A squatty, modern Tower of Babel, reaching not to the sky in an attempt to touch the pillars of Heaven but to the limits of man's technological genius.

Pride goeth before a fall. . . .

How often I had witnessed that over the years, pride in one form or another, pride that began with—

I speak the name with trembling.

Lucifer.

My master.

Even before Eden, before mankind caught the disease.

I shiver at the thought of him, the intent of him, shiver at all that has gone before, and all that he hopes to accomplish now with this grand dome.

Can demons cry?

I do.

*W*orkers are scurrying around inside, making last-minute preparations.

Two other men stand outside, looking at what they have wrought.

"We did it right," says the architect.

"My crew built what *you* designed," the contractor replies modestly.

"But *you* used quality materials," the architect adds. "Others might have cut corners."

"That's true," the contractor agrees. "But I guess it's because of this first convention. I wanted things to be just right."

"I know what you mean," the architect says. "To the honor and the glory of the Lord."

"We give them the showcase," the contractor muses briefly. "What they do with it is up to them."

They both fall silent for a moment, undoubtedly memories of the Evangelical Scandals of the 1980s still fresh in their minds.

"It's a really fine idea," the contractor acknowledged. "Build a convention hall, turn it over to Christian conventions of sufficient size, then rent it out for secular affairs the rest of the time."

"In the long run it will pay for itself," the architect said. "NRB wants to use it every January. NAE is just about committed. Even ABA is interested."

"That secular book convention?"

"Exactly. Real promising start."

"You bet!"

The two of them leave.

I think of what they said. It didn't *sound* so bad. The words seemed worthwhile. What could possibly be wrong with Christians supporting such an enterprise as this amazing building?

"Observer, come here!" that familiar demanding voice summons.

I turn.

DuRong is standing a few feet away.

I go to him.

"Record this," he tells me.

I acquiesce.

"This may be one of the greatest opportunities of all," he says. "Lucifer wants us to pull out the stops."

He makes a grand gesture toward the whole of the dome.

"They'll all be there, you know," he says. "Every major ministry, most of the minor ones—all the publishers, all the television and radio media. The first convention to be held there. How brilliant a stroke!"

I nod in agreement.

"The attention focused on them will be enormous," DuRong is jumping up and down with glee as he speaks. "We can peel up the layers that are so bright, so pretty, so holy, and show the world what is really underneath. Jim and Tammy will seem like St. Francis and Mother Theresa in comparison."

"Or Billy and Ruth," I venture halfheartedly.

"Yes, *yes!*" DuRong laughs. "That's a good one. Yes, like Billy and Ruth!"

He falls silent for a few moments.

"Why have we never been able to get to them?" he asks finally. "So many others, but not *them?*"

"Because—" I start to say.

"Go on, Observer. Because of what?"

I cut myself off.

"It is a very long story, DuRong."

"Tell me sometime."

"Yes . . . sometime."

*C*hristian Media Congress International.

The ultimate communications gathering in all of Christendom—scores of countries involved; nearly two thousand exhibits; an expected attendance of forty-thousand people.

It was not a surprise when Lucifer decided to make CMCI a special target!

We had a conference at a certain building that was a special gathering place for us in the Southwest.

"Remind you of something?" Mifult remarked as we entered.

"I have to admit that it does," I told him.

"Probably the same architect," he observed.

As soon as we all had gathered, Satan took the podium.

"I asked you to meet here because you are so familiar with this place."

At that we all had to laugh uproariously. I checked my notes from an earlier time, recalling the details of Arch Strutter, the minister Satan had seduced early in his seminary days.

All it took was three promises: 1) You will be paid a great deal of money; 2) You will become famous through your television ministry and your books; and 3) You will be able to build a monument to yourself.

Irresistible.

Arch Strutter fell for it and never recovered his previous evangelistic purity, which became ashes at his feet as he walked through them, led by the beacon of the seed faith which he now merchandised so expertly.

"What a warrior he has been for our cause!" Satan beamed, unconsciously strutting like pompous Arch Strutter himself. "That seed faith garbage has worked! But now we must expand our horizons, slow down with our attacks on individual ministries and plan something much bigger, where we can bring down *many* all at once."

"But I thought Swaggert and Bakker—" D'Seaver spoke up.

"We can do *better*," Satan cut in icily. "We can destroy a hundred *more* ministries, all at the same time."

And that was when he told us about CMCI.

The possibilities indeed were exciting to my fellow fallen.

The plan seemed devilish, in every sense of the word.

And here was how the master outlined it for us.

Representatives from the entire worldwide Christian community would be trapped inside the giant new convention hall.

"While that first *Christian* convention is in progress," he said, gleaming, "we will have had several bombs planted by an Islamic terrorist group. These will go off and cause further havoc."

As he pranced around and around on cloven feet, he added in other details, the structural weaknesses inherent in the hall from cut-rate materials, despite those earlier claims to the contrary.

"Even Christians can be bribed!" he shouted.

Yes, I thought, *money is a powerful tool for our cause.* I remembered the clergyman who decided that he would not eat a single morsel of food until his supporters sent in enough money to retire his ministry's debt.

I was there in the midst of his so-called strike. There was in fact no such denial of sustenance on his part; it was simply one of several promotional campaigns planned as part of an overall marketing effort.

"What's up for next time?" he asked at one of the staff meetings.

"We could rent you-know-whose prayer tower," someone offered, "but then he tried that gimmick once, stealing the thunder from you, I might add, and as we all know, it backfired on him."

Actually that evangelist had stolen nothing; it was the other way around. . . .

"I have a idea," said a young man who had only recently joined his organization.

"Let's hear it," the minister replied.

"We have you follow in Christ's footsteps and get a cross and strap you—"

"Wait, wait, wait," the minister interrupted. "We're not talking about anything real here, you know. I don't want to get too authentic. It's all a show. No place for—"

"The truth?" the young man interrupted this time. "Is that what you're saying?"

"Now, now," the minister said condescendingly, "you're new here, so I'll make allowances. But from now on, think Hollywood."

"In other words, what has truth got to do with it?"

"Exactly!"

The meeting in that very familiar building was nearly over. Everyone was excited.

"Do we need to vote?" the master asked.

"Nay!" we shouted as a group, as ever.

"Good," he said. "Now, go ahead and tear every damned one of them apart."

(Damned? Funny thing for him to say. . . .)

I was the last one to leave. The building was familiar indeed, for we knew every inch of it. There had been little to restrain us over the years. From the beginning, we were able to corrupt the very foundation of that ministry, as so many others, but this one was a particularly worthwhile success, costing as much as it did, money that could have been used to feed the poor, to pay for scholarships for Christian students, for a score of other purposes, all spent on monument to ego—a spectacular, wasteful display not of Christian humility, but of satanic excess.

I sighed as I went outside to join my demon brothers, turning for one last glance at the architectural and acoustical masterpiece (or oddity, another debate in itself), moonlight shimmering off the polished and shiny surface, off all that brushed aluminum supported on square steel girders, pane after pane shouting its silent blasphemy to the clear, cold night, and that huge stainless steel cross, weighing in at several tons, rather like the burden this earthly deceiver who founded that ministry will be shouldering when he finds his destiny is indeed not quite what he expected.

A great deal of care is put into making sure each booth is meticulous: the right layout, the right materials, the right book titles prominently displayed. Before the Christian media companies ever attend the convention itself, they plan, and plan, and plan.

"The lighting must be improved," someone says in a special staff meeting at one publishing house. "Last year it was a little suspect."

"I agree," the president of that company replies. "We mustn't have any dark, obscure corners."

Color is a critical ingredient also.

"Leave the garish stuff to the pennant peddlers," the president tells the staff members. "We should have earth tones."

"I like that display from those guys in Nashville," his sales manager adds.

"The rich mahogany look?"

"Absolutely. As classy as you can get."

The president rubs his chin. "Why not alternating sections of cherrywood and that lattice-type wallcovering in very light beige?"

They all agree that this sounds quite good.

The meeting is ended with prayer.

My comrades *hate* this part. It chases away any success they may think they have had in focusing attention on booth decor, convention scheduling, publicity material, and all the rest.

"When we have their minds on the nitty-gritty details," DuRong points out, "especially sales projections, we're able to tune out what they *should* be thinking about—namely, winning souls."

"Yet not even the apostles," I speak up, "ever tried to pretend that it was possible to be thinking of Him *every* second of the day. Watering the lawn needn't be an act of worship as such. Going to the bathroom can hardly be approached in any evangelical fashion."

"Yes, yes, of course, but—" DuRong tries to say.

But I will not let him get off the hook so easily.

"You have learned so *little!*" I spit the words out. "You try to claim success where there is none. It isn't a *sin* to plan what an exhibit at a convention is going to look like. It isn't even a sin to spend a whole week on that consideration. Where is your victory, DuRong? Tell me! Show me!"

"I have only *the master* to report to," he retorts angrily. "You take your little book and go off with your unsuspecting host and engage in your literary pretensions."

DuRong is correct, of course: I am the journalist on the battlefield. By and large the soldier demons tolerate me, but that is the extent of it. I record the victories, the defeats. I experience little danger. I exist on the fringes, of the human world and the spiritual.

And I long for the heaven that will not be attainable for any of us except by force. We keep ourselves going by dwelling on that goal. Some *enjoy* their silent reverie, relishing the prospect of Satan's taking over the throne of God, and sitting upon it, and making saints from all of history do his bidding.

We keep ourselves going. . . .

M'Eo had the right view of all this not too long ago.

"It is nothing more than an obsession," he remarked. "Yes, I find it fairly easy to admit that. But then obsessions have propelled men to victory for thousands of years. Why should we be any different?"

*T*he evening before the convention opens, everything is in place. Carpeting covers the concrete floor of the main hall. All the banners are in place. The cherrywood exhibit with the beige wallcoverings indeed seems tasteful. More so than those with multi-colored balloons and often cheaply printed bumper-stickers, one of the aspects of the modern Christian world with which Satan has had the greatest success.

Commercialization.

Some of it is unavoidable. But much is simply the money-changers-in-the-temple mentality that Christ temporarily exorcised some two thousand years before.

I remember the firm that one of my hosts worked for, its business simply generating new products. Not more *books*, because they weren't in the publishing end, but new *types* of product. And along with these came the need for names to give them, labels, product titles. I observed a planning meeting at one point:

Product manager: "What verses of Scripture haven't already been spoken for?"

Research director: "How about the one that talks about Jesus being a lamp unto our feet?"

Product manager: "Good! Now we have an idea."

Research director: "We do?"

Product manager: "Absolutely! We don't have any night lights in our line, do we?"

Research director: "I guess we don't."

Product manager: "Now we *will!* How's this for a slogan: *Let the Lord light your way at night.*"

Research director: "I really don't understand."

Product manager: "Picture it. A night-light in the form of a figure of Jesus. It'll sell like crazy!"

And it did.

There would be no such exploitation if there were no customers for it. Satan has always been masterful in taking sin and stretching it in one direction or another, often camouflaging it in a cloak of apparent holiness.

So many Christians are *things-oriented.* This achievement is one of my master's biggest successes, to be sure. In a society that is producing new cars, new electric shavers, new televisions, new computers at a rate that would have been unimaginable a few decades ago in a society whose advertising is the linchpin that holds all this consumerism together, it perhaps was inevitable that Christian industries would spring up that would endeavor to appropriate some of the "pie" for themselves, attempting to sanctify product-mania by a façade of reaching souls.

"The *world* has its stickers and gadgets and the rest," someone says. "What is so wrong with brothers and sisters in Christ grabbing a little of that? Every ministry needs revenue in order to survive. With products of whatever sort, we don't need to go begging for donations."

I think back to one of my hosts from nearly eight centuries ago, a contemporary of St. Francis. How strange that Francis of

Assisi should be known as Saint. For *all* who accept Christ in their lives are saints. But the appellation nevertheless does seem quite appropriate for this man. After he gave up his life of wealth, he established absolute poverty as his ideal. Early on, during a pilgrimage to Rome, he dressed in rags and joined the beggars in front of St. Peter's Basilica, begging alms from passersby and the well-clothed priests going in and out.

He had no committees to help him. He needed no majority vote. There were no marketing meetings. As I looked at this man, I felt an overwhelming desire to go to Satan and shout my disappointment with all that he had become, to say, "Look at this man! Look at his humility! He had wealth; he wore the expensive cloth manufactured by his father; he had power. But he gave it all up. He coveted nothing other than his Lord's approval. But *you!* You had everything, you had Heaven, and yet it was not enough. You were admired but not worshiped, and it was *worship* that you craved. This man has had long and painful illnesses, yet not once has he cried, 'Lord, Lord, why is it like this for me, one who strives only to serve You, to honor You?' Rather he takes the sickness, the pain, and *thanks* God for it as though it were instead a blessing of bounteous proportions."

I looked at this man, and then around at my master, so very different from the One who was clearly that of Francis of Assisi. I saw Satan rejoicing in the poverty of those milling about St. Peter's Square. They were dirty, they were hungry, some were sick; a few would die in the shadow of the immense wealth of that Christian institution before them, death that came from malnutrition while priests, clothed in silk garments, and wearing diamonds and rubies and emeralds on their fingers, dined on pheasant (I almost said peasant, which may not have been so inaccurate as a figure of speech!) and vintage wine, belching from rich sauces while they palavered about the intrigues of the day. Satan was as active in "religion"- then as he is now.

Seven hundred and seventy-odd years later, I stand not at the elaborate and beautiful Basilica but a new structure, and sense a similar dependence upon the material elements in life.

This is not the Vatican of today, with vendors selling water blessed by the Pope at a premium over containers of "ordinary" water, but it is something else, a Protestant version—

I smile with irony.

Martin Luther detested the hypocrisy of the Roman Catholic Church of that era, one aspect of which was the emphasis upon wealth, upon trappings of gold and gems and all the rest.

But now—

A few years ago, at other Christian conventions, the trend was only barely noticeable. Now it has become a flood, each new "Jesus Love Me" ping-pong paddle and its perversion of true spirituality bringing forth cackles of delight from my master.

As it would have driven Luther and Francis and others of bygone times to their knees, tears of shame flooding from their eyes, and pleas of repentance from their lips.

I leave my host for a bit. I have that kind of freedom, you know. I can stay inside each one. I can leave.

But, as I have said, I do need a host to write down my words, the words Satan wants immortalized. It is a Bible of sorts, pieces of which have been picked up over the centuries and used by dictators, Marxist rebels, drug dealers, murderers, the muddled-headed proponents of New Age idiocy, the crusading feminist lawyers who claim dedication to protecting the rights of *everyone* and yet concentrate on the homosexuals, the pornographers, the radical-types who are my master's favorite—the meat and potatoes of his spiritual "diet."

My book, my book. . . .

One that will never be on sale through CMCI yet their kind can hardly be blamed for not being a ready market for it.

I have every reason to suspect that Mao used some of it to deceive hundreds of millions.

It would seem that Hitler based his ideas on thoughts gleaned from the pages of my journal.

Anton LaVey's writings were another example.

And Shirley MacLaine's grand illusions.

The list is huge.

I may have the most plagiarized book of all time!

But it is not only other books that have been derived from the pages of my own. It is the thoughts uttered by those duplicitous politicians who try to present themselves as strongly committed to wiping out the drug epidemic, yet are unable to control the use of certain "substances" within their own household.

It is the reasoning behind pro-abortion bias in the judicial system.

It is every cop on the take, every mayor ever bribed, every judge supporting the rights of lesbian couples to raise children. (How pathetic the very assumption that those so deeply in sin have any rights whatever.) It is every Jim and Tammy Bakker whose actions have shaken the foundation of the entire evangelical world in the United States and elsewhere, as they blindly wallow in a cesspool of millions of dollars and limousines, and that twenty thousand dollar diamond she bought because she simply *tired* of the old one. It is all that paint around her eyes and on her cheeks and lips and in her hair, paint as much of the soul as of the body, those faucet-face tears coming from some polluted inner stream of greed and hypocrisy.

I like to believe that my book has provided the catalyst, carried on the backs of countless hosts over the centuries, whispered into the ears of kings and janitors, of stockbrokers and welfare recipients, spread by them like a plague into the lives they lead and the society they bring to its knees because of institutions built on sand and not solid rock.

But it's also the minister who beguiles his congregation with sweet words of specious redemption, of that which is purely personality and nothing deeper than that, not of eternity, a redemption not of Calvary but of Madison Avenue, not at the plain, roughly hewn cross of anguish and blood but one of molded plastic adorned by painted gold and fake diamonds, and offered as a "gift" in exchange for a donation "to keep this ministry on the airwaves."

It's a—

I walk outside the dome.

—homeless old man begging for food and—

I witness a little moment out of a little corner of Hell.

—being brushed roughly aside by a minister in a five hundred dollar suit, a contemptuous expression on his face as he sniffs sweat and urine in the air—

Hell?

—and in less than a minute the old beggar turns into a nearby alley, drops to the cold, dirty asphalt, coughs up a gusher of blood, and then dies.

That's right, I say.

I am suspended above the crowd, hovering unseen in the
air, going from one end of the hall to the other, aisle to
aisle, booth to booth. No one knows that I exist, no one
but the dying before they ascend to Heaven or descend
to join the other damned lost.

After a very long while, I encounter two who are genuinely
dedicated to the cause of Christ, as they put it, relatively young
men who have broken away from a larger book publishing firm
to form their own.

Their words catch my attention, and I stop to listen.

"Our second year!" says the taller, heavier one, his dark
hair a bit overlong for his age.

The shorter, slighter of the two, his blonde hair cut quite
short, does not speak initially, apparently recalling the events of
the past months, the struggle to get financing, the competition
for distributors, finding the right printing firm and then yet
more hard, hard work trying to persuade authors to give such a

new publishing company at least a hearing, and on top of it all, the process of staffing up.

"Praise God that we were able to make it to this point," the silent one finally spoke.

. . . *praise God.*

I am not surprised to hear those words at a Christian convention, but I am surprised that I haven't heard them before now.

I have heard about package deals. I have heard about marketing plans. And profit margins. Plenty of that sort of thing.

But not God. Not saving souls.

Until now. . . .

"You know, when we decided that we had to get away," the shorter man says, "we knew the Lord was in it."

His partner looks at him, smiling.

"There was nothing else we could have done," he says, "nothing at all."

They do not say anything else then because they are in public, and neither wants to be overheard by anyone of flesh and blood. But that night, in their motel suite, a great deal is made apparent in an emotional outpouring.

Their former employer was a man who believed in a tense, back-biting atmosphere within the office while presenting to the public a variety of sanctified-sounding book titles, including more than one dealing with Christian ethics and related subjects. His purpose was not to inspire anyone, but to force them to compete with one another in a variety of ways, even if this meant instilling a spirit of suspicion and jealousy.

The two finally could not tolerate it any longer. Though earning exceptionally good money by the world's standards, they were sickened by the practices around them, sickened by a level of conduct that was not a single notch above anything they had experienced in the secular business arena.

"It should have been different," the dark-haired one is saying. "It should have been kinder, more loving, more—"

"Money," the other adds. "That's what was on the pedestal, my friend, nothing more."

I find many publishers guided by The Great Commission. For these, books aren't simply conduits to a money stream but, rather, the tools given to them by God to reach the unsaved as well as edify believers.

Is there some surprise that I know the words that suggest sanctification?

If Satan can send out false prophets and counterfeit saviors, arming them with ideas aimed as pistols at the heart of the Body of Christ, while soothing the members of that body with words of positive thinking and related heresies that anesthetize them against the pain of the cancer multiplying inside, then he would be guilty of nothing more than guns with empty chambers if he had nothing to say that *rang* true while *being* false.

My master has studied Scripture far longer and more deeply than a whole seminary of students, no matter how brilliant they happen to be. He has every word of the Bible memorized. He needs no dictionary, no concordance, no parallel versions, for he was there when the first word was being written on ancient papyrus and he knows the latest paraphrase or translation. Only God has more of a grasp of Holy Writ.

A celebrity is autographing copies of his book at a special booth. He is wearing a watch covered with diamonds, plus an emerald ring on each hand, and a hand-tailored silk suit. He has just paid eighty-five dollars to have his hair coiffured.

"God *is* wonderful," he says as a broad smile crosses his face. "You can't outgive Him no how no way, brother!"

"Praise Jesus," says the middle-aged man who has just handed him a book.

"You bet, brother, praise Him all the way to the bank," the celebrity adds in a smirking, unguarded moment.

"What was that?" the man asks as he turns up his hearing aid.

"Nothing, brother, just a private little moment between me and our dear Lord."

The middle-aged man smiles. The celebrity sighs with relief.

And so I go on from there.

There are other celebrities, a few sincere, a few having earnestly repented of sin-ridden lifestyles and gone on to give Jesus *true* honor and glory, not the tinselly kind that is little more than empty hype.

But the rest. . . .

Ah, yes, *the rest!*

There is a book about a transvestite entitled *God Never Wanted Me to Be a Man!*

It is selling briskly, and has opened up the possibility of other books containing similar material. Two executives from another company have also noticed the newest bestseller.

"If Liberace or Rock could only have been reached for Christ, what a bestseller *that* would have been!"

"I agree. The marketing department would have had a field day."

"Publishing another book by Billy is boring. We need some real juicy stuff."

"We'll just have to wait."

"Wait?"

"For the next train from Hollywood!"

They both laugh.

I sense that the impressions which are forming in my mind cannot be representative, but as I go about the giant hall, I do see an increasing amount of commercialism, an assimilation of the techniques of the world—but not only that, the mindset as well.

And some within are aware, are concerned.

"I remember what it was like twenty years ago," observes a silver-haired gentleman seated at the CMCI main booth.

"Big difference?" a younger man asks him.

"Oh, yes," Silver Hair says. "It reminds me of what's happened to Hawaii over the years, how billboards and tourist trinkets and too many cars and too much greed slopped over from the mainland and threatened to destroy what had always drawn people to the islands in the first place. They were unique, they were unspoiled, they were a place apart where one could go to refresh one's soul. You can still do that in Hawaii but it's getting harder and harder."

Silver Hair waves his arm around at the displays that are on all sides.

"We've grown mightily, my friend," he says with a deep
sigh. "But we've begun to lose something along the way. You
have companies here that just don't belong."

"Like that New Age publisher?" the other says.

"That is *precisely* my point! They made it here by disguising their message with an evangelical *look*."

"What is worse is another firm, you know which one I
mean, that takes over a respected Christian publisher, pledging
autonomy while continuing to be the biggest of all publishers in
that entire New Age arena. How long will that autonomy
survive if Christian sales dip a bit, and books about mystic
crystals and some over-the-hill actress' reincarnation experi-
ences continue to set sales records."

Silver Hair is very pleased by the younger man's grasp of
the situation.

"Have you noticed the higher percentage of Jesus junk this
year?" he asks.

"I have," the other replies. "There's even a meter of some
sort to measure one's tongue-speaking ability."

"What's the principle on which it works?"

"Sound waves, I believe."

"The louder you shout, the more sanctified you are—is
that it?"

His friend nods sadly.

"You know what the worst of it is?" Silver Hair asks.

"What's that?"

"The secular media will do its job in here, and focus on the
junk, focus on the hoopla, and leave an impression that that's all
there is, that there is no real dedication to Christ."

"But that's not true!" the friend protests. "There are still
plenty of people here who care about what's happening, who
have their spiritual vision very much in focus."

An announcement over the dome's loudspeaker system
temporarily drowns them out.

"Tickets for the Mick Jagger Christian Rock Concert now
on sale!" the voice booms. "Get yours at booth 107D."

Silver Hair and his friend look at one another.

"When was *he* converted?" the friend asks.

"In time for his appearance here," Silver Hair says sardonically. "Tina Turner's supposed to have led him to the Lord."

His friend's mouth drops open.

*S*atan had a brilliant idea. But then he's sure that all his ideas are brilliant.

"I want to help a Christian journalist to do a book," he told us. "It will be an investigative look at what is wrong with the church today. It could sell hundreds of thousands of copies."

Oh? I thought. *What is the master up to now? Wouldn't such a subject be better handled by an enterprising young atheist on the staff of a major national magazine, someone with the instincts that would make him vicious enough?*

I found out my master's purpose soon enough, though at first blush it seemed that he had again succumbed to a certain madness that periodically roars about the lot of us all, threatening to swallow each and every one in its maw.

"We shall hunt for precisely the right one to research all the background and then to write it," he continued. "We shall open all the necessary doors, and he will be caught up in what he is doing."

"What are the qualities this writer must have?" V'Nity asked, logically enough.

"You will know him when you come upon him," Satan remarked.

Not terribly helpful, we agreed later as some of us gathered in the back room of a pornographic bookstore to discuss the matter.

"Where do we even start?" asked Mifult in a break from abortion duty.

"I guess a Christian college," I offered.

"Indeed!" my comrades shouted in unison.

And I was given the primary task of following that avenue, while others looked elsewhere.

So I tried college after college, "meeting" student after student, some of them quite bright, others rather dumb, none possessing the sort of impact that would make me realize *instantly* that he was *the* one.

Until I spent some time at a certain institution in the midwest.

A very angry young man was standing up before his class, expounding on a subject dear to his heart, but one that brings snickers from several of the other students.

"Christian psychology is a fraud," he tells them. "It is probably even a work of the devil."

How stupid! I told myself. *If it were that, a work of the devil, I would know far, far better than he!*

On and on he talked.

"It has its roots in secular humanism," he continued.

And some hymns have their roots in barroom melodies. Does that make them too profane for church use?

"It is being used to expound the most seductive doctrines ever to come from the master deceiver."

There you go again!

"Here's a quote from a leading Christian psychiatrist," Donald said as he picked up a book from the table next to him, and turned to a pre-marked page.

And what he read seemed devastating enough.

The students began to pay more attention to him.

"It really does say that?" a young man asked.

"I didn't make it up," Donald replied curtly.

He had them now. After class they gathered around, and talked, and he filled them with still more "information."

The book he quoted from was left open on the table. I looked over the same page from which he read. I repeated to myself the paragraph he used.

What? I said with a shout of surprise that no one could hear, of course. *How could he do that? How—?*

The paragraph was longer than the portion he quoted. And the second half put everything neatly into context, so it could be seen that the author was clearly severing all connection with humanistic psychiatry, *not* affirming its value for any *Christian* considerations.

In effect, he started out saying that the humanistic pioneers of psychiatry and psychology should be acknowledged for opening the door to a *way* of dealing with emotional and related problems of varying intensity—which is what the student read to others in the class—but that this was the sole value of what they contributed; virtually all the rest was the antithesis of Christian thinking, *the part that Donald conveniently omitted.*

Dishonest? Of course. That is what Satan loved about it. Such a tactic was old-hat with him, turning the truth into a lie.

*D*onald didn't give up. Donald kept on bending the ears of any who would listen. But it wasn't just a college pastime to him. He graduated, and went on into the so-called adult world while proselytizing about his views.

And he began to attract attention, not from those in his immediate acquaintance who always tired of his rantings, but rather from the Christian media. All it took was the most asburd statement of that lamentable group he had been making.

"C. S. Lewis is a closet apostle of the New Age!" he declared at a conference.

When presented with the facts about the hugely favorable influence for Christ that Lewis had been over the decades, Donald merely looked contemptuous, unwilling to be swayed in his views by anything resembling the truth.

Presto, his statement about Lewis garnered him major attention!

(A long time ago, Satan came to understand that he could set the agenda for the media, secular and Christian, just by getting someone to say something outrageously stupid or scandalous.)

And he merchandized that attention into a contract for a book with a top Christian publisher.

The stage was set for a bestseller.

It had everything, this book, scandal galore. When honest reporting wasn't dramatic enough, Donald would go off the deep end in favor of utilizing the same tactics as when he stood before that college class, supporting his ideas by deliberate distortion.

Satan had won quite an ally, quite an ally indeed.

The trouble is that many people, reading that book, assumed that he had done his job as a journalist, and that what he had written was rock-solid in its facts and such.

They don't know the truth. They don't realize how badly researched it was. So they accepted the error as gospel, if you will.

And this is where my master goes to town, as the expression is. The book sold hundreds of thousands of copies, each one read by three, four, perhaps five people. More than a million are exposed to material as legitimate as Ivan Boesky talking about integrity in the securities business; or Donald Trump preaching the Sermon on the Mount, especially the part about the meek inheriting the earth; or John Fitzgerald Kennedy doing a seminar on fidelity to one's marital partner.

If just ten percent, think of it, in excess of one hundred thousand people in America alone, were *influenced* by this book, and they did something about it, Satan's gambit could be seen for the master stroke that it was.

And that is just about what happened.

Many honest ministries were seriously hurt, especially in the charismatic sector, since a majority of Donald's targets were clergymen advocating speaking in tongues along with the prosperity doctrine.

The latter was the *single* area where Donald's rage was on target. Satan had long ago discovered that money and sex were among the biggest lures he could wave in front of the unsuspecting. With television and its celebrity preachers, he had the means of communicating the motive of hard cash to countless millions, Christianity by way of the local bank or savings and loan association, the depth of one's relationship to Christ characterized by whether there was a Chevrolet or a Mercedes in the driveway.

There was little else of worth in Donald's book, yet so many were duped into thinking that *everything* in the book passed muster as well.

No one can ever assume that, in leaving Heaven, Lucifer somehow left behind the intelligence with which the Creator had blessed him!

"It's the most dishonest book ever published in this market," commented a bookstore manager just before leaving to attend CMCI, where Donald is a guest speaker. "I only carry it because it sells, but I do keep it in the back of the store."

If it is so awful, then why not throw it out the back door? I shouted with words of piercing conscience unheard, and glad that they were not because I, too, am unable to serve two masters, though long, long ago, in dark and terrible moments of clarity, I know I have chosen altogether the wrong one.

Does Donald realize now that he is a pawn of my master, just as a murderer, just as a child molester, a pornographer, a ruthless drug maestro, regardless of whether their address was Bogotá, Colombia, or Beverly Hills, California?

There is no rifle in Donald's hands to mow down children in a schoolyard. He holds no knife. He sells no drugs.

He lies.

So simple, isn't it?

Lies vomited up out of the reeking cesspool of his own embittered hypocrisy.

Standard operating procedure for my master, Donald's master, in the final analysis, for if God is Truth, then this pitiable creature serves Him not at all. While engaged in the pretense of serving Him totally in his self-anointed crusade for integrity, he instead abets the purposes of Satan better, better than if he had declared openly what he was about, and then all could run from him, seeing him as he was to become, a foot soldier of the enemy of their souls; but not knowing, they wallow in their blindness at his feet, eating the spiritual junk food that he shoves down their throats, and begging him for more, more, more.

No one should be surprised, eh?

In the arsenal of the Prince of Darkness, such schemes are quite, quite effective; when purveying sin as he has done since the Casting Out, Satan always uses the most expedient of tools, deceit being the handle that fit them all.

I n the end, Satan loved that one book but hated quite another. It had an ingredient the first did not. Integrity.

Published by the book division of an old-line Bible college, it peeled up layers of evangelical hypocrisy and corruption as well as heresy, which should have been a source of demonic delight. But the result was an *honest* look at what was wrong within the Body of Christ, an impetus to do something about it, which Satan hated.

One of my master's most successful ploys has been for even well-meaning people, not to mention those who do not give a damn (a word for demons but not for the redeemed), to be seduced into misinterpreting and distorting Scripture, and for this to become a large part of the foundation for their ministries.

"I am a god," one of the deluded screams at his congregation. "I am as much an incarnation of deity as was Jesus Christ."

Angels weep, but demons gesticulate with satisfaction at stuff like that.

"You all are gods," he says as he waves his hand at the fools who sit in the pews of that so-called church, lapping up whatever he tells them because they trust him.

In a minute or two they all are on their feet, their hands held high, palms upward, as they shout, "Gods! Gods! Yes! We *are* gods!"

When the author of the second book tried to contact this wretch, he was rebuffed with a simple, "I stand on my record."

But it was that record that condemned him.

And yet he was not the only one.

There were others, some of which demanded an apology from the author.

The author refused.

"What am I to apologize for?" he said during an interview. "For testing the spirits? That is what our Lord admonishes us to do. For confronting the religious hypocrisy of our day? That is what He did—and remember, we are supposed to be as Christlike as we can manage to be. So what is it that I must reclaim in regret, as though never spoken, and indeed disowned in the process? What is it? Tell me."

No one did.

L *earning Tongues in Seven Easy Lessons! Don't Just Wait for the Greatest of the Gifts!*
Inside the meeting room in the basement of the convention hall, a man dressed in a turtleneck sweater is standing before a group of several dozen individuals.

"Your life can be revolutionized in no time!" he exclaims. "Each day can be an adventure."

It is clear that those present are intrigued, all except one man in the audience. He seems impatient. As the minutes pass, he shifts around more and more frequently in his chair.

Finally he stands.

"Sir?" he interrupts the speaker, who looks at him rather sternly but, with some reluctance, gives him the floor, as they say.

"I have been listening very carefully to what you have been telling us," he says. "Your words are very appealing."

The speaker nods with obvious appreciation.

"But, sir, I have two questions to ask."

The speaker waits, thus giving his consent.

"They are interwoven," the man in the audience continues, "so I will ask them together: How can you expect people to pay for your advice when the Bible says the gift of tongues is something God may or may not give to each individual? Does it not then cease to be free, something for anyone who completes your course, irrespective of what might be God's will in the matter?"

The crowd grumbles. The speaker begins to sweat profusely.

"Everybody's doing it," a woman shouts. "What's wrong with wanting the best?"

The man sighs.

"Have you taken any prophecy courses?" he asks.

"No, I haven't," she replies. "I'm not interested in what might happen in the future. I want what I want now!"

The others clap at that.

"Then surely you have studied the gift of teaching," the man persists.

"Not interested," she says as she folds her arms in a gesture of stubbornness.

"How about *any* of the other gifts, ma'am?" he asks with unfailing politeness.

Irritated, the woman stands and glares at the man.

"One other question," he says bravely. "How about love?"

"Love?" she repeats, momentarily puzzled. "What does love have to do with it?"

"If you were to speak with tongues, if you were to prophecy beyond compare, if you could teach everyone, and you did not learn how to love, it all would be for naught, dear lady."

"How *dare* you judge me!" she bellows. "How dare you try to impose your views on me! Where do you get off trying that stuff, *mister*?"

The man holds up his Bible.

"It's all in here," he says simply.

The speaker speaks.

"Leave this room!" he demands.

"Do you not want the truth?"

"Out! Out! *Out!*" they all shout.

He turns sadly, and exits to the corridor where I am standing, though he cannot see me.

"So sad," he says softly, "so sad."

The audience sits down, returning their attention to the speaker.

"And now here's the kind of profit you can make teaching others to—"

He brings out a chart littered with dollar signs.

I feel as sad as Darien must be when he sees this sort of thing.

Darien.

A kindred spirit in Heaven.

My enemy now.

We have met only twice since the Casting Out—when one of my hosts, a fellow playing a piccolo, had only minutes left to live; and in Hell, just before God accepted him back into Heaven.

How many of us wished we could have gone with him, could have forsaken that place of damnation and—

Not possible.

Never, never.

I remember a moment that was Darien's but which I desperately wished was my own, a moment unforgotten even for the length and the breadth and the depth of eternity. His words haunt me.

. . . *the hard rock shelf on which rests Christ's body. He is passing from death to life. . . . Finally He sits up, then stands, smiles at me, and says just five words, "Now you know the truth. . . ."*

"Yes, Lord, I know the truth," I manage to reply, barely able to say even that, aware of the moment to which I am witness.

A short while later, someone approaches from outside.

A woman.

Our eyes meet.

I find myself saying, "He is not here, the one you seek. He has risen, as He promised."

It is as though the light of Heaven is on Mary's face, her expression sublime.

I watch her go. My whole being weeps with the joy of redemption profound, purchased in blood for all of humanity and which included mercy for a foolishly errant angel.

A voice, rich, kind, familiar. . . .

"Darien, are you truly ready now?"

*"Yes, Lord, truly. . . ."**

Darien, Darien, if I could have done so, I would have stood by your side, and begged God, "Please, please, take me as well! I want no more of this cesspool that has been my existence for so very long. Oh, God, please!"

I should not have been called Observer. I should have been dubbed Hesitation instead, or Some Other Time, or whatever.

The moment passed.

As it always did.

Oh, how I hesitate before glancing in the next room.

"My dog, praise God, my dog was God's instrument of revelation," a burly-looking man is saying as he works himself into a frenzy before the crowd, and crowd it is, this room a bigger one, every seat occupied.

"I just knew as surely as though sweet Jesus Himself had spoken to me that when Sparkie barked, it was a sign from Heaven!"

If I were human, with a stomach, I would be sick.

I n each room in the basement of that building I encounter a different pitch, a term I had learned some time ago, and which seems altogether appropriate now.

I next hear a man confessing his sins of adultery before a very large gathering.

"I was led by Satan's lust to sleep with my employer," he tells them. "I threw aside my wife, and she dumped her husband."

There wasn't a sound apart from his own words.

"Her body proved irresistible to me," he went on. "That first night we spent together—"

I look around the room. Several men have flushed faces. The women pretend absolute shock but hang on every word. Only one younger woman gets up and leaves, muttering, "Trash!" The others seem not to hear.

And then the speaker holds up the $17.95 hardcover book he has written and reads a lengthy passage from it.

I block out his words, since he cannot be counted on to tell anything but his own self-serving side of the story, and I read

instead from my own book, because I was there, helping
D'Seaver as this man sank deeper and deeper in his shame. . . .

There was power in the way he spoke to the multitude, a
thousand men, women and children gathered in the auditorium, brought there by a testimony that had spread throughout
the Christian world.

"I obey Christ and Christ only!" he exclaimed. "He is the
center of my very being."

People got to their feet and shouted their approval.

"The Lord first and foremost, and all others next," he went
on, emphasizing yet again the central message of his books and
his personal appearances.

In the back of the huge hall, a man in his mid-forties has
entered but the crowd paid no attention to him. The one on
stage was the draw, not this rather mousey little man who
seemed terribly nervous.

He paused a moment, looking ahead, and saw the author.

The author, the newcomer told himself, *yes, and more . . .
the author, the—*

On stage, the speaker was coming to the end of his seminar.
For an instant, he caught a glimpse of a familiar face, and a chill
grabbed his spine.

"And may—may—" he said stuttered, following that face,
seeing the man walk closer, very near the stage now.

"May God cleanse your minds, your hearts, your—" he
continued through sheer force of will.

The newcomer smiled at him, and turned away from
the stage itself, to the side, to where the dressing rooms
were.

"—souls and those homes of yours, keeping them free
from—"

*How could he? How could he stand there? How could he say
such things, knowing—?*

"—Satan's corruption, and always, always, I say, always
strong and pure—"

Pure? Oh, Lord, I pray that you forgive him. I may never be able to do so. . . .

"—for Him!"

The crowd was on its feet, cheering again, as those listening had done several times that evening, their hearts open to the words of a man they had admired for many years.

Finally he walked backstage.

The newcomer stood there, in the corridor behind the curtains, saying nothing for the moment, but simply looking at him, smiling in a certain way.

"I don't know what to say," the author spoke. "I don't know what to tell you. I didn't mean for anything to—"

The newcomer said only one devastating word.

"Adulterer!"

Then he swung and connected with the author's jaw, spit at his fallen form, and walked away.

A man rushed up to the author and asked, "What was *that* all about?"

The author looked at him, then brushed past, and headed for his dressing room. After going inside, he sat down on a folding chair and started weeping. . . .

"Wonderful," loathsome D'Seaver cackled.

"I quite agree," another added. *"Are you writing all this down, Observer?"*

I was. I was.

It began with a million-copy seller.

And it ended in the bed of the owner of an important bookstore chain.

The book was entitled *Keeping Your Family Together through Crisis.*

This Mr. Robert Langworthy had been a top author for a very long time, his works selling into the hundreds of thousands of copies.

But he had not had that breakthrough sale until the latest title. The subject matter combined with his straight-forward way of dealing with it had struck a nerve in the reading public, and they responded with their pocketbooks.

Twenty printings!

"What an opening," Satan had told us at the time. "He will soon develop some arrogant pride."

"And pride will go before his fall," responded a demon who seemed immensely proud of himself with that burst of insight.

"Observer," Satan said, "Observer, copy down everything."
I did. I did.

His lover was not a beautiful woman in the classical sense. But she had a charm that Robert Langworthy found irresistible, and she exuded a sense of power that he simply couldn't ignore.

He was married.

So was she.

But somehow that didn't matter . . . enough.

I sit alone, looking back at the wreckage of this man's life. I watch him one day as he faces a bookcase filled with his literary works. I grimace as he turns it over, flinging dozens of copies onto the floor. I—
He stands before the pile, his entire body shaking. . . .

Robert Langworthy attempted to go on, to put his life back together.

In Minnesota he signed the divorce papers.

In Florida, his lover put the final piece into place in the destruction of her own marriage.

A week later they tied the knot.

Six months passed.

The Christian world turned its collective back on him.

He consented to an interview for a secular newspaper's religion section.

"Why don't they try to understand?" he said plaintively.
They did. And can't.

Finally a publisher took one of his books. And promised an
energetic campaign to re-establish his reputation. So he appeared at that first convention in the dome.
The book bombed.
The publisher did little to promote it. Of course, few
writers can be satisfied in this regard, seldom ever thinking that
their book has been "pushed" as much as they would like.
But it was different this time. The publisher just wanted a
name, no matter how tarnished. With some luck that would be
enough.
It wasn't.
Later, one of those who survived, at least physically, he
found that his phone calls were never returned, everyone caught
up with other matters of life and death, shorn of hypocrisy.
So he decided to start his own publishing firm, he and the
woman he loved.
That is, the second woman. Not the first.
"People out there do want to hear why . . . they want to
know that my attraction for this woman could not be tempered.
It grew. It grew daily. What was I to do? Maybe the Lord was
trying to tell me something. I had to listen."
Maybe. But he didn't.

It is soon all over now. Ashes to be trodden on and scattered.
Over, yes.
For Robert Langworthy. For his lover.
Not for me.
I observe. I report.

*F*ame had a great deal to do with it, you know. Fame twisted their world, and their minds along with it. But there are hundreds of thousands of *unknown* people, some of them wealthy, some of them "merely" well-off, people who have nothing more to cling to than the very bank accounts that they have been accumulating over the years. My kind have a field day with men and women such as this.

For them, it is dollars, not neon lights.

For them, it is trying to devise every tactic they can to keep *and* to increase the bottom line for themselves. And no matter how much they have, it is never enough.

But, going further down the scale, there are countless numbers who are not wealthy, who are not well-off, people who *yearn* to have a great deal of money someday, and who live beyond their means in lifestyles maintained by plastic credit cards and ever-expanding mountains of debt.

Hard times cause them to groan and wail and ask, "How could God do this to us? What is He punishing us for? What have we done wrong?"

Would you *listen* if He did answer? I ask of people who cannot hear me.

Would you give up your materialism and serve Him at any cost?

We followed Satan at the cost of Heaven.

Would you follow Him, whatever the price, *into* Heaven?

We gave up God.

What would *you* give up? A luxury car, perhaps? A diamond ring? An Oriental rug?

Odd, I tell myself.

What is odd? I ask myself.

I spoke that as though Christians would read it in my book, I answer. *But by the time they had done so, they would have been beyond choice, beyond redemption, those Christians who were Christians in denomination or church-affiliation only. The charade of their so-called Christianity would have been dust at their feet by then as they writhed in the grip of my kind, calling futilely for the intervention of a once-Almighty God rendered impotent by Satan's victory. Now why was that? Why to them? What good—?*

I pause, fluttering my wings momentarily, hoping fellow entities from Hell had not heard.

Truly strange. . . .

I come across one of the saddest cases of all—a brilliant success for my master but sad otherwise.

Philosopher's son.

Oh, how the father inspired millions. I was in the same auditorium as he was the night he died. So was Darien. How it all stands out in my mind! The wisdom he showed about so many subjects presented to him by the students in the audience.

And then at the end—

It is obvious that Philosopher is very, very weak. He walks slowly back to his chair, and almost collapses into it. His family whispers to him that he must stop.

"I must go in a little while," he says with great tenderness to the audience, looking out over the thousands listening to him. "I am grateful that you have come here this night. May we make the next question the final one, please?"

Another student, a girl raises her hands, and Philosopher asks her to come forward.

"Sir, as you indicated earlier, you once could not bring yourself to believe in God. I cannot now, either. Help me, please."

Philosopher speaks, but his voice is barely above a whisper. He motions her to come up to him. She climbs the steps to the stage and approaches him.

"I am dying, my young friend. Let me tell you that there is a God, and even as I speak, He is welcoming me into Heaven."

He looks at her, his eyes wide, a smile lighting up his face. He reaches out his hand, and she takes it.

"Your father says to tell you that he loves you, and is happy now."

Then Philosopher's head tilts to the left, the hand drops, and he is dead.

The girl starts to sob as she turns around to face the audience.

*"My father," she tells them, "died a week ago. The last thing he said—he—he said to me was that he prayed I—I—I would accept the gift of faith and—and—peace that he wanted to leave behind."**

That was Philosopher's legacy.

But what of his son?

His son is an angry little man, someone attacking the very foundation's of evangelical Christianity, often hitting the mark but just as often missing it.

He set himself up, set himself up as the conscience of the Body of Christ, abhorring compromise—

Abhorring compromise.

Oh, yes.

And loudly so.

That was how it started with Philosopher's son, following very much in his father's footsteps but hating the shadow in which he had to labor, hating the comparisons, resenting it when he was deemed to be falling short.

And so he constructed an elaborate deceit, one he came to accept quite totally, a rationale that would have filled Philosopher with disgust, but which seemed just right for him.

I hear the son talking with someone at his publisher's booth. He has just spoken at a rally the night before—and got a standing ovation—cleverly hiding some aspects of his outlook and giving the thousands in attendance only that which they wanted to hear.

"I live in the real world," he is saying. "When I hit my finger, I curse. When I see a beautiful woman, I lust after her."

Seeing that the man to whom he is speaking is rather surprised, Philosopher's son adds, "Do you think that *this* is the real world?"

As he says that, he waves his arm around to indicate the hoopla in the convention hall.

He is right, of course, and yet I know very well that he cannot use one circumstance as justification for the other. According to his viewpoint, then, all the rapes, all the murders, all the drug addiction, all the other social and moral crimes are part of the same *real* world, and somehow should be thought of within the same spirit of tolerance.

Years ago he raised money for a motion picture. And the whole Christian world stood up and cheered. The son of Philosopher would show what could be done when an evangelical Christian was in charge, the same Christian who did so well in exposing hypocrisy within the evangelical community.

The movie was *worse* than many of the non-Christian ones he had once protested against. It was riddled with four-letter profanity; it had gruesome scenes of revenge-oriented violence, revenge by the only Christians being portrayed; there was a gang rape sequence; and in the end, the moral of the story seemed to be that you have to kill your oppressor before he kills you.

The son of Philosopher had this defense: "I make movies in the real world."

(That phrase again. "Shame, son," your father would say. "Shame upon you for what you have done to your heritage.")

Weeks before, a Hollywood studio boss, a man fanatically hostile to Christianity, remarked in similar defense about his sex-ridden bloodbath of a movie.

What is the difference between the two? it might be added.

The studio boss is an unregenerate atheist.
Philosopher's son is a Christian.
That makes it right . . . doesn't it?
(Scorcese, are you listening?)

I am not alone most of the time at this convention, Milfult and DuRong and others are invariably there, in the aisles and at the booths and in the meeting rooms, taking advantage of any situation they can find. Often they come up against believers too solidly versed in Scripture and girded about with the Spirit of Truth for demonkind to make any·headway, rebuffing inroads my kind attempt by instigating the spectre of greedy motivation—which has collapsed more than one Christian business, indeed, *any* clever deal-making strategy that borders on the unethical.

But still they try, my awful comrades. It is good that they, that I, cannot be seen. We are hideous, deformed. The smell of disease is about us, our visages making us phantom Medusas, dripping with the foulness that we have accumulated over the ages, damned even if there were never to be a promised Judgment Day. Often we will rummage through piles of bodies on some foreign battlefield, trying to find those with yet a fragile spark of life offering some hope that, at the very last instant, we can divert someone, anyone from Heaven to Hell.

We do this to the pleasure of the master whom we serve with all that we are and will ever be. Often we are successful, several of us drawn to the dying one like vultures fighting over a morsel of meat. Finally, when he dies, and his soul is ours, we rip and tear as though at flesh, driven on by his screams. I no longer stand aside, watching, but drawn by the "taste" of what could be called spiritual "blood," I dive in with ferocity that never ceases to startle me in the aftermath. Remember, I am Observer, the quiet one, the demon appalled by much that is indeed demonic, and yet there I am, so ravenous that it seems as though I can never be satiated, my very being *requiring* the pain of the victim writhing at our attack. But soon he is relegated to Hell for even worse miseries, and how jealous we are because we can no longer be those responsible.)

I stand down the corridor from a large auditorium where the really important meetings, seminars, entertainment affairs are held. And I see an astonishing sight.

Mifult, DuRong, A'Ful, others are leaving in a mass exodus.

They look . . . frightened.

How can that be? What could make them react in such a manner?

I start to enter the auditorium. Mifult sees me.

"There was a reason why I wasn't allowed to abort *that* one!" he exclaimed, shaking nervously. "I didn't know what it was at first. All the normal excuses were present."

"I don't understand," I say quite dumbly.

"He would have been quite sickly. The parents could never have afforded the expense of caring for him. He would probably die before he was more than two or three years old, *if* he lived *that* long. And so on. And so on."

Mifult seems to be going through convulsions but after a few seconds manages to steady himself.

"Don't go in there," he begs. "You mustn't—"

But I ignore him, and enter anyway.

Every seat is taken.

On stage at the front of the auditorium are only two individuals, a fragile-looking boy and his mother. Even though the loudspeaker volume is on full blast, the child's words sometimes are difficult to hear.

"I am very tired now," he says, and rests his head on his mother's shoulder, and dies.

She continues to stand there though obviously trying to fight back tears that are beginning to drip over her lower lids and down her cheeks.

Suddenly there is the sound of voices raised in prayer. The hundreds of men and women in that auditorium stand and—

I see Heaven opening up.

It is not often like that, my eyes beholding the majesty of my former home. But this time I do, I see angels descending. They stand around little Robbie as his soul leaves his body.

And something quite wonderful happens.

Peace like a river attendeth my way. . . .

That is the expression on Robbie's face. Peace envelopes him, as water surrounded the baptized Jesus in the River Jordan. All that is finite, all that is corruptible, passes away.

And the Holy Spirit descends not as a dove—no need of symbols or surrogates any longer. *The Holy Spirit* takes the child's hand.

Robbie casts a glance at the crowd in that auditorium. Their voices are raised in praise, many with their palms upheld. He reaches out toward them and in a beautiful way touches each one, some driven to tears as they fall to their knees.

He hesitates but an instant as he looks at his mother that final, final moment before, someday, they walk the golden streets together. Her tears are a river of their own.

I love you. . . .

Not words at all. A sensation. Something rippling in the air perhaps, gossamer-like.

She senses it instinctively, raising her head toward the ceiling—and at the same moment there is a touch of fear because she also senses me, her expression suddenly dark, a last fleeting reluctance to let go, to acknowledge her beloved's odyssey.

Fear.

Satan's greatest of all weapons.

But I will not be his instrument this one time. I will not allow it *this* time!

I start to leave that auditorium.

It is well with my soul, mother, I can hear him say clearly.

And then he is gone.

She smiles as she raises the fingers of her left hand to her lips, kisses these, and holds them out to the empty air.

He is not there, dear lady, I say, yes, I say that. *He is*—

Home.

I find out much about Robbie through the discussions I overhear later. He appeared to be in better shape, temporarily, than he really was. The leukemia seemed to be in remission.

His mother had written a book about her son, a book with an implicit message that if she had known in advance about what would happen with his life, she still would not have chosen abortion.

"How many people have been touched by his courage?" she said at one point. "How many lives have been enriched because of him, mothers and fathers and children who could face their own ordeals with just a bit less emotional anguish? How many souls are in heaven today because the Lord used my Robbie as an instrument?"

Linked.

Yes, they were.

The mother knew immediately when something was wrong, even before he himself was able to tell her.

Except that day.

They lived in the city where the dome had been built. They had taken Robbie to see it in various stages of completion. He was fascinated, thrilled. He enjoyed talking to several of the men at the construction site.

He begged her to take him with her when she was scheduled to speak.

"I want to be there with you," he pleaded.

And he seemed stronger just a few hours earlier.

She had no resentment—and that made Satan livid.

Something else did as well.

The reactions throughout the crowd within the convention hall and in the meeting rooms.

For a short while, they turned from their books and records and bumper stickers to thoughts of a dying boy who seemed only a bit tired and who put his head on his mother's shoulder for the last time.

None saw what I did.

For many it would have meant a total change of everything they were, of every aspect of their lives. How could they any longer *care* about trinkets and feel-good pep talks and other banalities? How could they not see beyond the cheap and easy answers to what mattered for *eternity*, instead of getting lost in the TV dinner mentality of today?

But for me, there was nothing of the kind, no redemption of outlook, nor any other aspect of my existence, for that matter.

A dog returns to its own vomit, you know.

*A*s I go up and down that huge convention area, I hear the whispers about little Robbie. His death there in the basement of the dome has had a striking impact that goes well beyond that one room.

I see a man crying.

"What's wrong, Alfred?" his wife asks.

He is sitting in the midst of their booth, which is filled with banner stickers, key chains, erasers with Bible verses printed on one side, notepads and other items. On an easel to one side is a sign about special CMCI discounts. Earlier Alfred had worked hard to close a deal with a major Christian bookstore chain, bargaining at the top of his form, and succeeding. He would make a huge profit from it since most of the merchandise was bought in the Orient at very low cost.

"All this," he tells her.

"I don't understand, Alfred."

"All this *junk!*"

"You've never called it that—" she started to protest, then stopped, realizing that they both knew what they were doing, what they had been doing for years, selling stuff that took the name of Christ and *used* it, not in any honest manner, not in any *real* attempt to evangelize, to spread the Good News of salvation through Christ and Christ only, but to make money, to see a bottom-line profit at the end of each fiscal year.

"That kid, Robbie," Alfred says, "I was *there*, Evelyn. I stopped in for just a moment but that was enough."

He wipes his eyes with a handkerchief.

"He had no regrets. He didn't curse the Lord. He showed only love and trust. And it was the same with his mother. They were so beautiful, Evelyn."

He looks with contempt about the booth.

"What does all this amount to? What does it contribute, Evelyn, except money in our pockets?"

He holds up his wrist.

"A gold Rolex. People are being killed for ones just like it these days. It's worth thousands of dollars. I pay a hundred dollars for a pair of shoes and don't think twice about it. But that woman, that boy, they had to struggle for the money to keep him going as long as he did. They had to beg for whatever they got. But I just bought a thousand-dollar suit because I'd always wanted one!"

He starts sobbing, loudly.

"Please!" Evelyn says. "People will see you!"

People do.

But they have other business. One little man in one little booth is really of no concern. They have their own problems, including finding the right titles for the Christmas selling season.

"What's wrong with that man?" a woman asks as she passes by.

"Who knows?" replies her female friend.

They both laugh at the poor fool.

And then they stop an aisle or two further down.

"We shouldn't have done that," one says. "Maybe he's going through some kind of tragedy."

Her friend nods in agreement.

"Let's go back. Let's see if we can help."

In the coming holocaust, those two will be among the injured. The poor fool will come upon them, and kneel beside them, and hold their hands as they cry out their pain.

Behind him, far down at the other end of the convention area, his booth will be in shambles, pencils and banners and everything else spread out in a hundred directions.

"Where is your wife?" one of the two women asks as the pain momentarily abates.

"I don't know," he mutters. "I don't know. She was heading for the rest room when—"

The woman reaches up, touches his cheek.

"We know what matters now, don't we?" she says. "There are no excuses anymore."

He nods.

*T*here is another young Christian whom I encounter, much older than Robbie, whose story has an altogether different ending. . . .

He seemed happy, this babe in Christ, as he was called by those around him.

"We've lost another one," DuRong had said.

"Yes, as far as eternity goes," A'Ful replied, "but we can still do a lot with him here."

DuRong brightened up considerably.

"You're right!" he exclaimed. "Any plan?"

Indeed there was . . .

The young man, Erik, left the football stadium where the evangelistic meeting had been held, feeling light-headed.

"I'm clean," he said, "washed clean by the blood of Jesus."

He returned to his dorm at the college, ready to take on anyone he encountered.

His roommate was amused.

"You actually fell for that stuff," he said, smirking.

"It's not stuff," Erik protested, "it really isn't."

Arthur is sitting in a chair, looking up at his friend.

"I've never seen you this way before," his roommate admitted.

"I've never *been* this way before," Erik replied, "too many problems in my life, so much guilt, as you know all too well."

Arthur realizes how true that was. The two of them had spent long, long hours, days, weeks of conversation, revealing to one another their deepest possible thoughts, emotions.

Erik had gotten into drugs, and along with this, prostitution to finance his habit.

It went on for years. No one else realized what was going on—that is, the respectable people in his life, the ones who belonged to the normal part of his world—no one except the drug peddlers and his customers.

"I hated everything around me," he said. "I hated snorting white powder up my nose. I hated the depression that came each time after a 'good' session with the stuff."

He was shivering, sweat sticking his clothes to him.

"But . . . but I just couldn't stop," he continued. "I was hooked in every way imaginable."

Wanting to isolate himself from the possibility of guilt creeping in, he became more and more a part of the sub-culture that cocaine inevitably spawned where it took hold. If there was no one to tell him that his habit was wrong, that it was destroying him, he would never, he thought, have to face up to the reality of what was happening to himself.

And there was the sex.

He had flings with many women. With street hookers. With politicians. Even the wife of a minister.

"She never took off the cross she had hanging from a chain around her neck, not even when we were in bed together. I felt so dirty . . . so dirty."

But eventually the drugs and the danger of AIDS, which he tried to ignore but couldn't, drove him to seek help. With his family by his side, and Arthur as his friend, he was able to turn his life around and break away from the old habits. But he still suffered from the guilt these left behind.

"I actually liked what I did," Erik would say. "I *liked* the idea of sex without restraint. And I got *paid* for it all. I could live out my own fantasies through fulfilling those of my customers."

Fantasies.

What a helpful word, what a devastating set of circumstances used by Satan to entrap any who stand before the open door to Hell!

People have their twisted erotic fantasies because Satan has had his own!

Every sin known to man was first foreshadowed in Satan. Sin cannot come from God. God is total purity, total good, total justice.

Erotic sins are not exempted. Satan has known lust an inordinate number of times. He expresses it through surrogates.

But at least once he intervened directly. I remember it well. Even the Scriptures record it.

He had his own form of Immaculate Conception. He sent his followers, a horde of demons, to earth during the period just prior to the Flood, and had intercourse with loose women of that time. This was only part of the display of evil and sin in those days, but it was typical, and it was what drove God to judgment.

Have there been other times?

The answer to that question would require me to start another volume, which I cannot do, as it becomes increasingly difficult for me to continue with the present one!

"Then, with the money, I could buy more drugs which I imagined made me more sexually voracious. So I got further and further into sado-masochism and made more and more money that bought a bigger and bigger supply of—"

That stage passed, the confessional part of his rehabilitation. He never again went back to drugs, to paid sex. But he still could not salvage any degree of self-respect.

That was when he happened upon the evangelistic crusade, and attended the service that night in the stadium.

And then he could say, with utter certainty, "My sins were washed away! They really were. My guilt is still there but I feel better equipped to face it, deal with it, *conquer* it in time!"

His roommate listened carefully, and as his skepticism faded, he found what his friend shared with him to be more appealing that he might ever have imagined.

And soon he accepted Christ into his life as well. The two of them began attending a church that is located a couple of miles from the college.

Erik felt literally like a new man. And so did Arthur. They in turn witnessed to others. But, one Sunday, they decided to try a new church, because the one they had been attending began to feel a bit staid, a bit narrow in its outlook. The new church was a number of miles from the college, but the day was a pleasant one, the drive a welcome prospect.

They were ten minutes early for the morning service.

People gathered around.

"Where are you from?" a middle-aged man asked.

They told him.

"Good! Good! Praise God!" he said.

The man's wife remarked, "We're having a praise service today."

They smiled, though a bit uncertainly.

The man picked up on this.

"Anything wrong?" he asked. "You do speak in tongues, don't you?"

"No, I—" Erik replied.

"You *don't?*" the woman said. "What a shame! What a shame! Now we're going to have to do something about that, aren't we?"

Both young men were led away from the main auditorium, down a couple of corridors and into a "special" room.

"This is where God tells us it is to take place each time," a tall, thin man in his mid-forties told them.

"What is that, sir?" Erik's roommate asked.

"What is what, son?"

"About what you said, I mean, that something is going to happen here?"

"You will receive the baptism of the Holy Spirit."

"But I thought that that happened when we were saved."

The man and several others in that room broke out in laughter.

"You *do* have a lot to learn, don't you?" he said, chuckling.

And then it began. These people were more aggressive than many others in the charismatic movement, but the bottom line was the same. To be legitimate, to be accepted, these two young men *must* have the Gift.

That is one of Satan's most seductive heresies. It is also a direct copy of the tactics he used in the Garden of Eden. There was nothing illegitimate about the Tree of the Knowledge of Good and Evil; God put it there in the first place. But His clear admonition was that the fruit was off-limits. Adam and Eve were *not* to eat of it, period.

But Satan changed all that, planted doubt in their minds, made them disregard God's unmistakeable command.

And sin entered the world as a result.

"We can do it again and again, in one form or another," Satan has been telling us throughout the ages of history. "It worked once, it has worked other times, and it will continue to do so because of man's sin nature."

And now in the twentieth century he is finding continued success; this time it is not a legitimate tree as the tool but a legitimate gift that is at issue, that has been at issue ever since Paul wrote to the Corinthians.

"The difference," he says, "is that God is not telling Christians they *can't* have it. He is saying that He *wants* them to be blessed with it or—"

He raises himself up proudly.

"—perhaps prophecy, healing," Satan continues, "or one of the others."

We are back in that church in the Southwest; we feel comfortable there.

Our master is at the podium, gestulating.

"*But,*" he says with special emphasis, "God adds one condition: that they wait on Him, that they do not covet after one particular gift but simply depend upon Him to bestow the one that *He* knows is right for them."

Satan starts to cackle, a cackle we are very familiar with, and which over many thousands of years has never ceased to fill even us with a certain dread.

"*But they don't!*" he exclaims. "That is the secret. Adam and Eve couldn't wait to do what God forbade. And today, all this time later, they fall for the same old trap. I almost feel that I should try something new, but then why? *This works so well, as you can see!*"

God tells Christians to wait. But they don't. They are lured by the promise of the Gift, brushing aside the other possibilities. They have services, they have classes, they publish books, they produce cassette tapes—all geared toward *getting* the Gift from Him.

Is a gift, any gift, in fact a gift in the truest sense when it is *demanded* by the recipient from the giver?

And yet countless thousands of Christians are increasingly beating on God's door, as it were, begging Him, pleading, insisting that the gift *they* want is the Gift they feel He *owes* them somehow.

"So foolish," Satan tells us. "They are so blind."

And we cheer. We must. Satan *needs* that. The vanity that forced him from Heaven *demands* our acclaim.

"As we all know," he continues, "tongues indeed is a perfectly acceptable gift that can bring about a changed life for those upon whom God chooses to bestow it."

He speaks from raw experience. There have been innumerable times when he was so close to claiming a soul forever, when he had that individual drowning in defeated living, and yet someone introduced the possibility that tongues might be the answer, and there was much prayer, much seeking after God's will, and finally the individual was given the Gift, and their life was revitalized as a result.

"For such people, tongues was the answer," Satan adds. "And for others it has been the answer as well, and the cause of our defeat."

He pauses, then says, slowly, *"But so can it be with any of the other gifts if the recipient is wise enough to give God the honor, the glory, the gratitude, and realize how miraculous all such intervention is from the Creator Himself!"*

Satan is proud that he can speak the language as persuasively as any clergyman from any denomination.

And with the gift of tongues, he is, in the current religious climate, having a field day on both sides of the fence, as the expression goes.

His plan is simple. There are many, many thousands of Christians who, coveting no single gift, have been blessed by God with the ability to speak in tongues. And they have tried to understand this new dimension in their lives, to use it in a way completely in accord with Scripture.

Added to this group are the ones who seek only personal gratification, for whom tongues is nothing but a kind of pep pill to be used when they are feeling low and need an emotional lift. It is a mark of exclusivity, something that sets them apart, something that seems to make them *special,* even in comparison to other Christians.

And against these two distinct varieties of charismatics are set the fundamentalists, the conservative evangelicals who are repelled by the excesses epitomized by the second group. They understand the scriptural invalidity of the way a precious gift has been taken and distorted in its application to daily life. Some even say that such a gift was never meant to be continued beyond the era of the New Testament writers. And thus the stage is set for fireworks.

"Ideal circumstances!" Satan says in exultation.

Warfare of a sort ensues in the Body of Christ, a cancer that can spread throughout, dividing congregations, splitting denominations, tearing apart families!

Making it more insidious is a not-so-minor detail.

It may be that God, forgiving as always, will give the gift of tongues to some who are *demanding* it. It may be that the beauty of the gift, the joy of it, the edificational basis for the *true* gift as detailed in Scripture proves to be just what they need to cleanse lives that have been lurking in the spiritual shadows.

But there are many today from whom God has turned aside in refusal for His own good and holy reasons, who nevertheless *seem* to be speaking in tongues anyway. They continue to glory in their undecipherable utterances, boasting of this gift to anyone who will listen, tricking many in their ignorance and dragging down their lives into a cesspool of "I have it, and you don't, and that makes me a far better Christian" pride and judgmentalism littered with the landmines of doctrinal error, planted by my master, and ready to explode.

Satan has the ability to counterfeit virtually everything that is of God. He did it in the medieval period when the Roman Catholic Church became so bloated with the lard of its own power and importance, temporally and, Catholic theologians purported, eternally as well, blinding the various popes and priests and others to the multiplied error upon error that had risen up like stinking excrement around them.

He has done it other times over the hundreds of years since then, both within Catholicism and the Protestant denominations. Now, it is the Evangelical Scandals of the 1980s that have born fruit for his demonic designs.

"Think of it," he tells us all, "most of them are charismatics!"

He would wave that before the noses of those who are so obsessively anti-charismatic that they become jubilant when they hear of anything that causes skepticism about the *entire* movement, people who were not above using the charismatic thread that ran through the Scandals as a weapon—and with some success—never realizing that ministries having nothing to do with the movement also would be hurt.

"When one old woman who, too ill to go to church, spends her Sundays watching the heavy guns of the Four Square Church or Assemblies of God on television and suddenly sees those in whom she put her trust shown to be hypocrites or worse, it will be an H-bomb blast exploding in the very belly of Christianity," he adds, "because she is not going to be alone. There will be other old women as well as old men who will be so disturbed that they will turn away in disgust, unable to extricate themselves from the maze of betrayal in which they find themselves.

"But it's not just the elderly. Housewives in their twenties, thirties, and forties will find it almost impossible to watch a Christian program without some doubt, some question, some skepticism. I will play on this; it will be my foundation. And upon this foundation will I build the kind of apostasy that will precede the advent of the Antichrist!"

He is nearly beside himself.

"It is so *wonderful!* The carnal ministers, the ones mired in the filth of their private lives are the ones who will get the headlines. The other charismatics, the decent, honorable ones who try daily to live their lives by the guidance of Scripture, none of *them* will garner even a moment of media time!"

And he is correct. Satan is often correct. If that were not so, if his plans went awry most of the time, he would amount to a pathetic and emasculated foe. Whatever remarks can be said about my master, and hit a bullseye as far as truth is concerned, that is not one of them.

... *the ability to counterfeit virtually anything that is of God.*

There have been apparent healings that are not healings at all. What about the preacher who supposedly cured people of brain tumors, arthritis, bad hearts, and more by grasping their foreheads and throwing them backward? Whenever he wasn't doing that sort of thing, and anyone wanted to talk to him, all they had to do was go to the tomb of his dead wife where he prayed by the hour, and claimed to have gotten advice from her in the process!

Satan is very good at taking grief and making it something obsessive, driving people to mediums and weird cults. There has never been a medium, male or female, whom Satan has *not* controlled.

And then the cults, including the Church of Latter Day Saints, Jehovah Witnesses, Scientology—ah, yes, that group of spiritual perverts, people who base their worship upon the idiotic ravings of a man whose science-fiction career was on the skids and who was told by his agent at the time, "Hey, Ron, baby, why don't you start a new religion?"

Regardless of any pious pretensions or façades, they *all* are instruments of my master, through and through—part of the darkness of the End Times (and Satan knows this, though he disputes how it all will end up!)

There have been other miracles that Satan has duplicated. When Scripture says that the spirits are to be discerned, to see whether these are of God or the devil, God was speaking with compelling force. After all, a good counterfeit hundred-dollar bill can deceive many. If men are capable of such, then think of what my master can do.

Often, I have observed, charismatics are guilty of failing to heed what Scripture says about testing the spirits. As a result, Satan is pleased indeed with the victories he has had over the years due to a seemingly minor bit of manipulation that pays impressive dividends for him.

"Get them to feel disturbed or, as they say, uneasy in the spirit," he once remarked. "You do that to a charismatic and you can practically smell defeat in the air—for them, not us."

I asked him to explain in more detail what he meant.

"Many charismatics fall consistently into the trap of thinking that when they have this 'uneasiness in the spirit,' it is a bad thing. So they claim the—"

He stopped, trembling a bit, unable to say *those* words. But I knew what he meant. The blood . . . *His* blood.

"—and that is supposed to do it," he continued. "They develop a ritualistic approach they think comes from spiritual courage and discernment, but it is instead a sign of outright cowardice, even spiritual blindness."

"How so, master?" I probed.

"If I suspect that they are on the verge of receiving some compelling divine truth, one that can give them new insight, and clear away the cobwebs of the old, I oppress them, I probe their sin nature. I—"

"*You,* master?"

"Well, you know what I mean—either me or one of your comrades. Now do not interrupt again. Understood?"

I agreed that it was.

"I bring about some kind of dark mood, some fleeting feeling of depression, and then I have them. They have been tricked into thinking that because they do not feel up, up, up, that because their mood is dark, sinister perhaps, that they have to reject whatever it is that God is trying to tell them, assuming, I suppose, that divine revelation flies into their lives only on wings of sunshine and light, without ever realizing that storm clouds can be of God also! What I have done, in these instances, is to short-circuit valuable truths."

Satan was quite satisfied with himself at that somewhat convoluted but unerringly accurate insight.

"It is a perfect situation, Observer," he added. "Make a special point of that in your book."

I assured him that I would.

*E*rik was in his dorm room. Both he and Arthur had been traumatized by the events at that new church. I wanted to see if Satan's plan was working, so, true to my nature, I observed Erik every chance I got. After what seemed like a very long time, he convinced the men at that church that he could speak in tongues. They heard the sounds coming, and, on this basis alone, without any analysis beyond that, their reaction was immediate, and effusive.

"Praise Jesus, praise Jesus," said the man who had prayed with him, "praise His holy name!"

There was much back-patting, congratulating, and finally, the man added, "Please consider us willing to open our church to you *anytime*."

Arthur, however, had not spoken in tongues, and he was ignored, pointedly so.

"I felt like a leper that they had tried to cure," he said later, "but failing that, they were determined to pretend that I just didn't exist."

As it turned out, neither had Erik himself spoken in tongues, which he revealed to his roommate on the way back to the college that afternoon.

"But they were *sure* that you had." "It *sounded* as though you were saying everything they had been—!"

Erik's roommate was surprised.

"You were just going along with them, weren't you?"

Erik nodded.

"I had no idea what to do," he admitted. "I just imitated that other guy."

"And he didn't know the difference," his friend muttered.

. . . *he didn't know the difference.*

That was the scariest part for Erik. If *he* could fool them, who else could do the same thing to those individuals at that -church, perhaps others far more evil than young Erik?

*U*ltimately, Erik began to doubt his salvation. He read a number of books about the subject of speaking in tongues, but became more and more confused. Going to several other charismatic churches didn't help.

Until he found one nearly a hundred miles away. Arthur didn't go with him this time, nor had he gone to most of the others. He was changing. He was drifting, disturbed by the incident in that church, the phoniness of it, phoniness raised to a level of sanctification in the deluded view of those who had tried to force him to speak in tongues.

After the service, which didn't include a demonstration of the Gift, as the others had, Erik walked up to the pastor, an elderly and sincere-looking gentleman named Harold Forrester.

"Sir," Erik said at the entrance as they shook hands, "I have a real problem. It's about this speaking in tongues stuff. Do you have any time?"

The old man looked at him kindly, nodded, and motioned for Erik to wait until he had finished shaking hands with the remaining members of the congregation. Then he took Erik outside. The day was a pleasant, sunny one.

The church was located in the middle of farming country, and there was plenty of open acreage all around them.

The scent of manure, pungent, filled the air.

"I love it here, Erik," the old pastor told him. "I wouldn't know how to live anywhere else."

He stopped at a tree trunk, an old one.

"It occurred for me right here," he said. "I was on my knees before the Lord, leaning my arms against the top, and suddenly I spoke in what we call heavenly language."

He turned and looked at Erik.

"But there was no joy!" he remarked, with a somewhat mischievous grin curling up the corners of his mouth.

Erik was stunned.

"But I thought there was *always* joy," he said.

"That was how I myself had approached the subject. I had been trying for years to get the Lord to give me the Gift because I *wanted* to *feel* that joy."

"But why then? When you were least expecting it?"

"That, too, was a question I wrestled with, Erik. I chewed on it for hours afterwards. Finally I called a friend of mine who had been speaking in tongues for some time, a fact that I frankly envied about him. So we got together at my apartment. And we were both on our knees, praying, when I spoke again in tongues!"

"But without any joy, I suppose," Erik says, sure that that was what had happened.

"Oh, *no!*" Forrester told him, his whole expression changing as the wrinkles of age seemed to recede a bit and there was something that could only be called a glow about him. "I've never experienced anything so intense—the greatest jubilation imaginable, Erik. It was the complete opposite of the first time earlier that same day."

He saw the frown on Erik's forehead.

"You see," the old man said, "my friend *understood* the words. It wasn't gibberish to him. He *interpreted* what I had been saying. And that triggered my joy, my profound joy.

"That was why the apostles proved to be so ecstatic on the Day of Pentecost. There they were, before thousands of people, from as many as a dozen countries, and speaking nearly as many languages. Peter, John, and the others saw before them the first mission field they had encountered since the death, burial, and resurrection of Christ, and yet at first it seemed impossible that they could ever communicate, simply because they didn't know Chinese or Greek or whatever other language the people spoke."

"But God gave them the gift of languages on the spot?" Erik asked.

"He did, he did indeed. And, later, when they talked about that moment among themselves, they were nearly overcome with the impact. In fact, those who heard them thought they were quite mad or quite drunk or both, because they acted with such abandon, and this was because never before in their lives had they felt so close to God, so touched by Him. It was a clear-cut moment they could point to that showed his intervention from the spiritual world into their world, the world of flesh and blood."

For a short while, Harold Forrester seemed not at all like an elderly preacher but a very young one indeed.

"Can you *imagine* how that must be, Erik? To sense God reaching *into* your very being, and taking charge of your vocal chords, and all of a sudden you open your mouth and you are speaking what *He* wants you to say!"

Abruptly his shoulders slumped. Erik was concerned.

"Sir, are you all right?" he asked.

The minister nodded slowly.

"From joy remembered in days of youth to the despair of this era," he remarked, "quite a journey, my young friend."

"I don't understand."

"Let's go to my study. I'll *show* you what I mean."

They walked back to the church, and Erik followed the pastor to the little study, its shelves crammed full with books and magazines.

The elderly minister searched for several publications and spread these out on his desk with a grunt of disgust.

"Look!" he said. "Look at that stuff."

What Erik saw was an assortment of garish covers, with blaring headlines, often "colorful" stories, and a number of photos of familiar celebrities.

"They've Christianized sensationalism. Or maybe they've sensationalized Christianity. How offended the Lord must be! Publishers have turned a holy and wonderful thing, the bestowal of a gift from *God*, into just another circulation-boostering gimmick. But they couldn't do it without the cooperation of believers themselves, without the eagerness shown by certain groups or denominations."

He tapped the covers with contempt.

"I could open the pages of more than one publication and show you ads for mustard seeds from Israel, gram bottles of water from the River Jordan, Protestant prayer beads blessed by a bozo named Reverend John, or some other embarrassment to the Cause of Christ.

"As disgusting as that stuff is, the worst is the space given to pronouncements by famous figures and the utter garbage that is tolerated from their lips or their pen or their computer, as the case may be.

"Some of them can proclaim God's admonitions regularly, or so they say, and be guaranteed premium space anytime they want, even when what they offer is foolish and, yes, injurious to the cause of Christ, if not on doctrinal grounds, then because they make some other crazy claim that sets them up for yet another round of ridicule."

He turned around, and walked over to one of the bookcases.

"It's the same there," he said, spitting out the words, "people blathering about what *they* think is the legitimate application of tongues and a hundred other subjects. Most don't know what they're talking about."

He sighed, deeply, something more than a sigh, actually.

"Everything has been cheapened these days," he said. "Worship used to be done in a quiet little place with a few people, the outside world sealed off, and not intruding. But mega-churches changed that, and television provided the death-knell. Now you have some actor or another getting up before that guy's congregation, you know the one I mean, and giving his testimony!

"Oh, the speaker may very well be a very nice man, maybe even a highly moral one up to a point. But I question, I seriously question whether most of these celebrities are people to be holding up as an example before millions of viewers. No one should be an example held up before others who is not a sincere, Bible-believing Christian! Some of these guys may be okay in the board room or on a music hall stage or a motion picture screen perhaps—but they just don't have any business standing up before a *Christian* audience. No one *else* belongs *but* men, women, and children who have fallen on their knees and sought redemption from the only One who can ever bestow it!"

"Some would call that a judgmental, bigoted view, sir."

"Yes, *some* would. But Christianity is a very exclusive religion. There is one basic requirement, the acceptance of Christ as Savior and Lord. An actor can treat the family dog as kindly he wants, with an ocean of kindness, if that were possible; someone else can give every cent he has to charity— and *still*, despite everything else that may be so wonderful, and fit the world's definition of goodness, they *are* headed for Hell if they haven't taken Jesus Christ into their lives. It's as simple, as profound, as unequivocal as that!"

*W*hat the old preacher said was quite true.
... they are headed for Hell if they haven't taken Jesus Christ into their lives.

Who would know better than those demons whisking lost souls from their mortal trappings, and depositing them among the inhospitable coals?

My master is *always* looking for ways to thwart salvational truth from entering the lives of human beings everywhere.

With the prostituted use of tongues, or what he has tricked worshipers into *thinking* is that wondrous gift, he has surely found one of the most enticing, compelling traps so far.

Yet it is but one out of a common cesspool.

Healing is another entrapment for the unwary. Crusades organized around this theme are usually filled with people, many of them desperate, who try to circumvent the capabilities of modern science and medicine and invoke the miracle of healing directly from Almighty God.

God has not lost the power, of course; but I know very well that He will not be forced into healing as a public display, healing-on-demand.

. . . *on demand.*

How utterly presumptuous it is to *demand* anything of Him. Satan tried that while still in Heaven, and we all suffered as a result.

Healing is a gift, as is tongues, as is prophecy, and the others. When gifts are *demanded* of the Heavenly Father, He is likely to bestow nothing at all.

Sometimes, though, He will heal in the midst of the carnival-like atmosphere of such a service. He will intercede from the infinite to the finite and show that of which He is truly capable.

Sometimes, yes, but not often.

Still, an hour spent at one of the crusades would give the impression that more than 90 percent of those who *are* touched by this evangelist or that one are healed.

Untrue.

Most find their physical condition virtually the same after the adrenalin of the moment has passed.

What about the evangelist with the hidden microphone being given information on the sly that, to the congregation, seems as though it has been divinely implanted?

And the people planted in the congregation that have little or nothing wrong with them but put up a convincing act as they become "miraculously" healed?

A vast array of deceptions.

Sewn together with a common thread that draws the gullible to them.

Addiction.

It is a word much in circulation during these last decades. Cocaine, marijuana, heroin, the rest—all have been well-reported. Yuppies use them, so do street gangs, entertainers, high school students, others.

Yet I have found that *Christians* are as addiction-prone as the coke-head delinquent who sells drugs to support *his* habit!

Most don't snort white powder through their nostrils, but their addictive tendencies drive them onward ceaselessly as they scramble to get whatever they crave for their own particular situation. They gobble up the worst tripe imaginable so long as famous personages dish it out in sermon after sermon, in books and magazines, on cassette tapes and compact discs, a vast so-called information industry having sprung up to supply their habit, a habit that chains them to the heretical "feel good" doctrines that are proliferating—to Satan's delight and God's dismay.

Lambs to the slaughter.

And that they are, pushed by the obsession to be up, up, up all the time. Chemically-dependent people pursue "up, up, up" through drugs. Christians do so by submitting to the clutches of religious opportunists who understand that the same societal tendencies that have made the drug epidemic what it is also motivate those who would never buy so much as a single joint of maryjane.

"Forget all that bad stuff in the Bible," one or the other will say. "We're past that now. We've *matured!* Holiness is happiness, happiness is holiness. If you're not happy, you're not holy."

People listen.

People grasp and grope and grab to fill in the vacuums that exist in life. That is, after all, why the whole shepherding nightmare started, and, also, how so many have been able to garner so much success.

"Let me take your hand," the unwary are told. "Let me mold your new life in Christ. Listen to me, and only me. God has sent me to—"

And so on, and so on.

The problem is that Christians are among the most gullible of all people—and the most dependent. There is little difference in the gullibility factor of Germans being seduced *en masse* by Adolf Hitler because life has become tense and hungry and insecure—and those Christians who are roped in by any preacher with a message that sounds as though it will be satisfying, no matter how specious it might be from a scriptural standpoint.

Can tricky pastors be compared to the new Hitlers in the resurgent neo-Nazi movement?

Absolutely.

My master is involved with both!

Both deceive, both are deadly. If anything, the influence of the Bakker-types of the evangelical community is perhaps worse than the influence of the Metzgers of the white supremacy underground.

Since I am a demon, I know firsthand how many innocent lives are lost through the racial hatred espoused by the various Aryan-type organizations. But many of the victims are Christians, their redemption guaranteed—which does not mitigate in any respect the injustice, the torment in this life, but it does mean that they are now where no more hatred can touch them, where they will share without end in the love of God, basking in the radiance of His glory. Oh, how I envy them!

Yet the preachers with false words from their lips and extorted money in their wallets create an *atmosphere* of redemption—but that is all it is, as vacuous as the air they breath. People believing they will go to Heaven are instead greeted by my kind in Hell, no beautiful chorus awaiting them but the shrieking, discordant fury that is their eternity.

Woe to you, wolves who take on the garb of shepherds! Woe to you all when we get our talons into you with special delight!

To squash a human soul!

To brush aside the hand that reaches up toward God and direct it in worship toward yourselves!

Palms upward, oh, yes, that remains part of the illusion, but with piles of greenbacks and a plea from doomed lips, "Take it, take it! *All* of it!"

To make them happy in the midst of this blasphemy.

To wrap around them positivity principles, principles from deceived minds who have pulled the wool over the eyes of countless thousands of Christians, with their recycled and thinly veiled humanism.

To brainwash them with the delusions of seed-faith principles.

To anesthetize them to what they really need to be doing, not grabbing at the manmade confections that look so sweet, but to get down on their knees, and let all the pus and gangrene and slop that has been building up inside them rush out in a confessional surge by admitting, finally, that there is *nothing* positive about their lives because they have been grasping at lies instead of deep-down-straight-from-He-Who-is-the-only-Source-of-it true truth!

And then when you get caught, as the expression goes, you weep and cry and say to the world, "The media are out to get us. Christians, unite against the devil's children."

But you are those children.

*I*f I were a born-again Christian, and not a condemned demon—and there is a wide, wide gulf between the two—if I were a Christian, especially one with influence, there is at least one television preacher I would concentrate on trying to throw off the air, and though there are others as well, somehow this one seems among the most targetable, because he is in such flagrant disregard of the norms of Christian worship and witness.

He is white-haired. And pot-bellied. He insists upon holding up before his followers the fact that he has the freedom to chomp continually on a cigar, if he wishes.

So I motivated my latest host to call his 800 phone number, and ask a single question: "Since unassailable evidence now exists that smoking causes cancer, lung disease, and other ailments, and since the Christian's body is the temple of the Holy Spirit, how can you justify your preacher's apparent addiction to cigar-smoking as a proper witness and not instead a stumbling-block to thousands of the brethren?"

At least that was what my host *intended* to say.

The flunkie at the other end hung up on him mid-way through.

Thinking that my host's true allegiance was the issue, and that the person representing the preacher had somehow sensed this, I had my host persuade someone who really was a born-again Christian to make the next call.

"I've been a believer for more than a quarter of a century," the Christian said.

"Praise God!" the rep replied. "How can I help you?"

"I fail to understand how a constant montage of shots showing your preacher's horses parading around to the accompaniment of rather raucous bar-room music is anything that could be considered edifying to the Body of Christ."

Again the Great Disconnect. (Not the Great Commission, of course.)

This Christian was irate. So he called a second time.

"Doesn't it bother your arrogant pastor that worldly music of the most unseemly sort is inappropriate for a Christian program?"

"He doesn't see it that way."

"He's not bothered by the offensive nature of that stuff?"

"Are you one of those offended?"

"Yes, I am.

"He cares not one whit about your kind."

"What *does* he care about?"

"Only what *he* thinks is right. Anything else is unimportant."

"Even if it contradicts Scripture, even if—"

Yes, another disconnect.

How anxiously my master awaits an opportunity to seize upon the moral and theological weaknesses in *that* ministry and exploit them just for the hell of it. But then he may not have to do anything else. People of that bent are pretty good at ultimately discrediting themselves and the Lord they supposedly are serving.

*H*ow many of the flock whose sins have entered the province of what is called "public knowledge" and supposedly repented of those sins have been able to rebuild their ministries and go on, as though nothing ever happened?

From the standpoint of divinity, shall we say, it is the very core of why Christ died for the sins of mankind. Those sins are actually forgiven before they are ever committed. They are *forgotten* by God, and the repentant sinner stands before Him cleansed.

Demonkind are continually tempted by this forgiveness, just as human beings are tempted to commit the very sins that then must be put under the crimson flow at Calvary.

If any of my fellows were, themselves, to accept this forgiveness, then Satan's empire would collapse overnight. It is the same with humans; that forgiveness breaks Satan's power over them. Humans have done so throughout the past two thousand years, while demons never have.

How ironic that the creatures feared by countless millions of men, women, and children are, in this regard, far, far weaker than the ones they would seek to torment and subjugate! It seems we are *bound* to Satan, too cowardly to risk his wrath, and yet lowly man has again and again proven courageous enough, faithful enough, to break those chains of domination and become free, free forever.

But that very forgiveness, in the case of straying televangelists and other Christians of significant public recognition, represents a big opportunity for Satan in such matters, upon which he can easily capitalize.

How does the flock *know* that the confession of sin is *genuine*? How do they know that it isn't merely for public consumption while the heart, the soul, of the individual is anything but repentant?

There is a booth on the convention floor with magazines and books being presented by one such ministry. The evangelist in question was involved in the sin of adultery with prostitutes; he had slept with not just one woman of the night but many of them, even though the public became aware of only the one, and it was only *that* one to which he confessed. He said nothing about the others. Was his broadcasted confession intended as an oblique umbrella for *all* the moments of sin, of consorting with whores in a dozen cities while he was on his crusade tours? Or was he clever enough to admit to *just* that one, knowing that attention would be deflected from the others and, with any luck, those would never be found out?

The question remains: If he did not publicly *acknowledge* the rest, did he privately come to the Lord and, on his knees, ask for forgiveness? If not, was his public admission of lust only a public relations ploy to save some scraps of his ministry so that these could be pieced together and he could continue, after a seclusionary period of time, right along as before, filling to overflowing the luxurious building bearing his name?

The doctrine of forgiveness is at the same time God's greatest blessing and an opportunity for Satan the Deceiver.

That doctrine is pervasive, so central to the faith of Christians
everywhere that when someone confesses sin, when someone
claims forgiveness, when someone jumps up and down and
proclaims cleansing as a result, then his brothers and sisters in
Christ tend to *believe* him, taking comfort in such phrases as
"Well, after all, that's why Christ died at Calvary, isn't it?" or
"We can't judge because only the Lord knows for sure, and we
have to accept such matters at face value, don't we?"

But it has happened before, of course; it has happened in
the case of a well-known writer of prophetic books who got
involved in an extramarital affair many years earlier, and he had
to go into hiding for awhile. But, today, he is back as strong as
ever, and more than one publisher is offering a book by him at
this convention.

If his repentance was genuine, then his new legitimacy
within the Christian community is something that shows the
strength and beauty of the Christian approach to life. If that
repentance is not altogether honest and true, then it can be
viewed only in one light: a device to get back into favor so that
he can continue to earn a living.

But how does anyone know for sure?

If only God Himself has the answer, then no finite man or
woman can possibly be certain.

But it is not just God.

My master, this chief of all demons, this Lucifer the Fallen,
also knows. He also is alone with such a man, evangelist or
writer or whomever, either through his appointed demons or,
if he takes a special interest, directly himself—alone in moments
when the public is a long way away, and there is no one else but
himself and his conscience and all the truths that either have
been played out before the crowd or kept in a private little corner
of his mind, his soul.

It is then that God knows. It is then that Satan knows. It
is then that the truth is apparent.

And in the case of the evangelist, in the case of the writer,
in the case of so many others who have *seemed* to be different,

to have turned their lives around, in these cases, cleansed as they supposedly were and so fine in the minds of their adoring Christian public, Satan stands rejoicing at the deception, counting the dirty secrets yet remaining, counting each one, and looking at those who gather before their celebrity leaders in trust and listen to what they have to say, read what they have to say, and proclaim, "We welcome you back with open arms, we have faith anew in you."

If they only knew.

*E*rik has paid for a one-day pass.

I watch him as he stands at the entrance, looking at the huge hall, with its three-score rows of exhibits, banners hanging from poles, the sounds of thousands in attendance, just like himself, music blaring from several directions.

"On Christ the Solid Rock I stand. . . ."

He catches those few words, but the beat isn't the same as with the old hymn that he had heard years before as his grandmother hummed it to him. The arranger had added an electric guitar, and the vocalist sounded like a cross between Elton John and Billy Idol.

Erik walks about, picks up an occasional book, leafs through the pages, then puts it down.

Someone taps him on the shoulder.

He turns.

"Can I help you?" the short, heavyset man asks.

"I was just looking," Erik replies.

"Could you use some pencils?"

"I—I don't think so."

"They're engraved with Bible verses."

"Does that make them holy?"

"No, it doesn't but—"

"But what?"

"It's a great fund-raiser."

"Why?"

"Isn't that obvious, young man? Because people will *read* the verses. These are *Christian* pencils, after all."

"Will they?"

"Will they what?"

"Read the verses?"

"Oh, yes!" he replies, anxious to get beyond that point. "My pencils are a bargain. And we're offering a convention special. An extra 12 percent off the retail price."

"A cheap way to witness, is that it?"

"If you say so, buddy. The cost per—"

"Are you making a profit?"

"Sure I am. Anything wrong with that?"

"Are you a Christian?"

"What does that have to do with anything?"

Erik is silent, just looks at the little man.

"This is a great market, you know. Just a few thousand stores grossed more than two billion dollars last year."

"What about soul-winning?"

"Soul-winning?"

"Yes."

"Whadda I know about that stuff? I'm Jewish. For Christ's sake, I gotta wear a cross to sell in here?"

Erik walks away.

He is tired. He feels a little sick. He hasn't been feeling too good for a while, now. Not since—

*E*rik is convinced he has no choice.

The joy he knew so briefly is fading fast. He felt uplifted somehow when he had talked to that old preacher in the country. But here, with all these Christians who hardly seemed inspired at all, except about money, he felt confused and angry. *Is this what Christianity is really all about?* he asks himself. *Is this all there is?*

Even here he has heard again and again the argument about the Gift. Some of the new books he has leafed through have said that he can't really be saved it he doesn't speak in tongues. He wonders if he is a Christian at all, because he knows he doesn't have the Gift.

He looks within his mind at the old images, that lifestyle of sex and drugs that had once grabbed hold of him until he no longer wanted to live if he had to spend one more day in one more strange bed, snorting from one more plastic pouch.

"I can't go back to that," he whispers, not caring whether anyone hears. "I can't go back to that cesspool. And yet the old minister seems to think—"

(D'Seaver is by his side. I hear him whispering the lies in a rancid stream, all the reasons why Erik should do what he had decided earlier to do.)

Don't listen to the old fool. He is just another phony, another hypocrite. As soon as you left, he was probably chuckling. They always do, you know.

"But he seemed so genuine. He seemed to know—"

He doesn't know a thing. His mind has turned senile.

"But he used Scripture. He tried to show me that tongues were a wonderful gift but I—I didn't need it to be—"

You do. You do! Don't be deceived. If you don't speak the heavenly language, you cannot be sure of your salvation!

"But I—"

Listen to that inner voice. There is no hope for you. You are doomed to wander on the fringes of lives more happy than your own. They won't accept you unless you have the Gift. You don't have it so what is there left for you?

"But Jesus will forgive me."

How can you be sure?

The elevator is packed.

He takes the stairs from the ground floor, to the second, to the third. Someone bumps into him, a middle-aged woman.

"Are you all right?" she asks, greatly concerned.

He tries to get away from her but she persists.

"You don't look well, son," she says.

"I'm damned," he tells her.

*E*rik stands at the railing on the third floor.
The vast hall spreads out below him.

It's all right, Erik. You've done your best. Look at the light, Erik. The light beckons. It's a soft light. It's warm, Erik. Reach for the light and it will surround you. It will comfort you. The light is everything. Believe in it, Erik. Let the joy overwhelm you.

He reaches out, freon-chilled air against his cheeks, sanctified rock music staccato in the background, banners flying, faces turned upward, pain as flesh meets wood and plaster and cardboard and then concrete, people rushing forward, a montage of their shocked expressions, someone's bad breath, laced with a hint of tobacco.

"I'm damned to hell. . . ." he whispers as his mouth fills with blood.

How sad, they say. Troubled young man, they say. If only someone had reached him for the Lord in time, they say.

No more light.

D'Seaver cackles.

*T*he reactions have been immediate, of course. The booth wrecked by Erik is an expensive one, and elaborate. It cannot be reconstructed for the remainder of the convention. The publisher is trying to be sympathetic, but he is also extremely upset. Crucial sales may be lost in the interim.

Massive confusion dominates. Even so, despite worries, order forms are being whipped out, and quantities of product are being sold. Even in the midst of tragedy, the show must go on.

But that is as it should be. Satan will not admit this. He would like it to be viewed as callous, insensitive, a clear indication of the paucity of true spirituality that has come to characterize such trade shows, as they are called.

Wrong.

He is very wrong.

As important as the life of one young man named Erik happened to be, no ministry, no publishing firm, no Christian educational institution, no convention should be allowed to grind to a halt, as the expression goes. If that were the case, then my master would have an easy way of it. All he would have to do is engineer a few dozen tragedies at the most influential Christian organizations, and the entire Christian community in the United States would be so traumatized that he would have golden opportunities for making headway, driven onward by the scent of victory.

So *this* show *does* continue to function, in fits and spurts, taking a little while to regain its momentum. And always there is discussion, sanctified gossip about Erik, with some of the details of why he did what he did gleaned from television interviews with a number of fellow students.

Two men are having a heated exchange in the cafeteria section of the hall.

"It's the way tongues as a gift is twisted these days by you crazy charismatics!" one is saying.

"That had nothing to do with him taking his life!" the other retorts. "He was a troubled young man."

"And this heresy put forth by the emotional screwballs abounding in the charismatic movement was the gun that they put to his head. All he had to do was pull the trigger."

"The *trouble* is that none of your Baptist churches gave him what he needed. They painted a picture of tongues that made this gift from God seem like a work of Satan's."

"The counterfeit is precisely that. It reduces the concrete reality, the truths of Scripture to a level of ecstatic gibberish, and what is left is utter theological nonsense—just the sort of vacuum that Satan favors!"

"*Your* problem is that you have become a dried-up shell," one of the men shouts. "God gave us emotions. God doesn't expect us to keep them bottled up, as though we are to be ashamed of having them in the first place."

"That's *not* what I'm saying, my brother. I *am* suggesting that emotions can be manipulated by the Arch Deceiver. I don't propose that the gift of tongues is invalidated today. I just offer the possibility that it is misunderstood and misused much of the time."

"Your attitude is the same as the Lord experienced two thousand years ago. You and all the others who look with such disdain on charismatics are guilty of a modern pharisaicalism that is closing the door to salvation for countless numbers of people."

The first man leans across the small square table until his nose nearly touches the other man's.

"And that is the greatest fallacy of all: the way you and the other loonies have gotten hold of isolated portions of scripture and twisted these to satisfy your own limited view. Speaking in tongues has *nothing* to do with closing the door to salvation *or* keeping it open for that matter. You all have meant needless guilt for thousands, perhaps hundreds of thousands of born-again people who keep striving for the gift, and when they don't get it, they begin to doubt themselves."

And so it goes. They don't end up physically assaulting one another, but there are moments when they seem not far from this extreme.

Finally, though, one apologizes for the insults, and the other apologizes for his anger. They stand, embrace one another, then go their separate ways.

Satan lost that one.

Satan loses many such moments during the convention. He tries so hard to get men and women to have their theological arguments or debates, and then attempts to build up a permanent barrier between them, a wall of festering feelings that is, in a way, as solid, as impenetrable, as anything physical.

And while there are successes, while he does cause pain in the Body of Christ, while the carnival-like hawkers of cheap trinkets and other such merchandise seem to be proliferating, there are the firm, the steady, the properly-motivated pockets of genuine ministry. These are people whose primary purpose is to reach souls for Christ, and books and magazines and plaques and posters are the means they have chosen, people who lament the intrusion of hoopla at the altar of sales, sales purely for profit, with souls saved as a byproduct rather than the reverse being true. These dedicated servants, appalled by what they see, become ever more determined not to succumb. And so, ultimately, Satan has lost another round.

And he cannot abide this. He simply cannot.

So he calls in the artillery.

Literally.

S atan got them to do what they did through hatred, their Muslim fanaticism already incorporating the "Americans are devils" mentality that led to the capture of the American embassy in Teheran, and so he had had to exert little persuasion for them to make the leap into something on the scale that he had in mind.

It has been fashionable in some circles, particularly those with a humanistic bent, to label as prejudice any attempt to call the Muslims or the Buddhists or the Hindus "heathens." But that certainly is what they are. Their religion rips from the Iraqis and the Libyans and the Iranians and others any façade of civilized behavior, any semblance of humanity, and makes them instead barbarians of the worst sort, ruled by men for whom no atrocity is too repugnant so long as it serves their delusion of a worldwide Islamic kingdom—which, I must add, would be nothing more than another version of Hell.

No one realizes this more than Satan and the rest of us. In fact, we are *more* aware of the evil dimension of fake religions, the

counterfeit cults, the mystical Eastern heretical sects than *any*
evangelical Christian, because demons are responsible for their existence in the first place, by which we have deceived untold millions.

But it is more than that. No Christian who has ever lived
and died in Christ has even a small fraction of the knowledge
about Satan that *we* do, simply because we have gotten it from
the source, Satan himself. That needs to be said. And I can see
with clarity that is profound, truly, truly profound how corrupt
the Muslims are by the very nature of their beliefs, beliefs aided
by demons for the sole purpose of increasing the harvest of souls
for Lucifer the Fallen.

Any religion without Christ is spiritually bankrupt. But it is
the Muslims who seem to be the most twisted, the most
maniacal, the most evil, paying homage to a leader who was the
worst kind of Satanic puppet because he seemed so good, so
righteous—but of whom we all had total and absolute control.
It is ironic that they hang a death sentence on Salman Rushdie,
the commendable author of *The Satanic Verses* when they are
the ones, as far as eternity is concerned, who are condemned,
and just not condemned, I say, but condemned to Hell. They
are the vipers of the world of flesh and blood, and I, for one,
rejoice when they find themselves in damnation forever, crying out
for the forgiveness that they so vehemently deny so many others.

That we must depend on these scum is appalling—but
then we use whomever we have to, murderers and rapists and
homosexuals and pornographers and feminists and hordes of
others, so it shouldn't distress me that Muslims are part of this
squalid list—yet it does, it always has when such as the Muslims
and the Scientologists and the Mormons and others of their ilk
rope in the innocent and never let go until the flames of the pit
of eternal darkness entrap seducers and seduced alike. (Christ
would not have used the word *scum* but then I am afraid that I
have absorbed more of my master's mindset, his very words,
than I have been willing to admit through the centuries.)

There had been plans for more than one terrorist strike
within the United States for some time. The first had occurred

months earlier when an American president had died of natural causes while still in office. Just as the British prime minister was entering the main air terminal outside Washington D. C., a little girl approached.

She is standing alone near the front entrance to the airline building where a delegation from England is scheduled to arrive.

Dressed in clothes that make her seem a harmless doll, she is holding a rather large handbag. Every so often she looks up at a passerby and smiles.

At the opposite end of the building, a British Airways plane lands. A total of twenty members of Parliament disembark. The Prime Minister and her husband are also on board, but she has had a slight case of airsickness. The others wait at the gate.

"She is supposed to be made of iron," whispers one of them.

"Please, Harold, do not be sarcastic," an associate responds. "You try to hide how much you really do admire the lady, but despite yourself, you cannot."

The other man is silent.

In a few minutes the couple joins them, and surrounded by security guards they head toward the entrance. The Prime Minister seems quite recovered, walking with a sure step.

As the party approaches, the little girl runs up to the first member of the delegation, and gives him the handbag. She is smiling with the sweetness, the innocence of the very young.

"Please, mister, my mommy—"

She is unable to finish.

An explosion demolishes a large portion of the building, pieces of it scattering for nearly a mile. Most of those directly inside are killed—as well as many more on the outside, bodies flung in a dozen directions.

Several times the number of those dead are injured, blinded by shards of glass, flesh torn by metal, limbs severed, bones broken.

"A war zone!" says the U. S. Government official observing the scene.

And that it appears to be. The terminal in ruins, girders twisted like a toy erector set abused by a very angry child. . . .*

*M*y master couldn't have been happier about the chaos at the air terminal. He stood amidst the wreckage, saw the broken and twisted bodies sprawled in a dozen different directions, saw the prime minister on her knees beside the man she loved, and laughed.

"Glorious—" he started to say until I interrupted him.

"Why was this necessary?" I asked him.

"You tolerate the murder of six million Jews but the deaths of a dozen or so makes you question the wisdom of my actions?" he said angrily. "I fail to understand the significance, Observer."

"Is it possible that you go too far from time to time?" I asked, a little of my insolence already dissipating against his intimidation.

"If there is pain, if there are questions such as 'Where is God in situations such as this?' how *can* there be even the remotest chance of going too far?"

Satan was licking fluids from the festering sores on his lips.

"I used to hate the taste," he said, distracted for a moment, "but now I rather like the bitterness. Would you care to sample some, Observer?"

I backed away, repulsed.

"Better yet, since you are my servant, I command you to kiss me on the lips, taste the pus, tell me what you think of gangrene, Observer!"

As far as humankind is concerned, we are beings without substance; some go even further and call us nothing but the insane fantasies of the religious right perhaps. (How successful we've been with *them*!) But when you are a demon, well, it is altogether different. Just as dogs can hear sounds that humans cannot, so can we see what man does not until the moment of death. We can do all manner of abominable acts among ourselves.

I wanted to pull away. I wanted desperately to rebel. I wanted to throw him aside, and go begging to the gates of Heaven, not just because of what he had asked me to do, the humiliation of it, the disgusting filth of which I was being called upon to partake, but also, and mostly, because of the crumpled and battered bodies sprawled all around us, because of a little girl's skirt stained with red, her flesh shredded by the force of the blast and a multitude of glass shards, because of the most powerful woman in the world, not caring who saw her in the sudden surge of grief that bespoke her utter helplessness, she who had the power to start a great war virtually anywhere on the planet, was now reduced to a near-hysterical level of wrenching grief, her power meaningless in the one way she would have chosen to use it just then if she could, if she could.

None of this shamefulness *had* to happen.

None of it would mean the difference between success and failure in any of the planning hatched in the mind of Satan.

There was simply no *justification* for this latest monstrous deed, though I wondered why this one had affected me so, for it really was just part of a perverse tapestry woven out of the bones and veins and other innards of the countless victims of his rage.

Yet undeniably I *was* overwhelmed, as though I stood before the battlefield of Armageddon, witnessing hundreds of thousands of bodies, some not quite dead, their hands raised toward a stormy sky like stalks of marsh grass in a bloody inlet— a moment we all knew was yet to come, and about which we often thought, surrendering to the delusion that the dead were Satan's and by no means God's. And so the sight of spilled guts, the more the better, should in fact precipitate our rejoicing, and against such a panorama, stretching on, it seemed, to the very horizon, the sight of a few limp forms and some twisted metal and a child's dismembered doll, none of it should begin to compare, none of it should have the impact of Armageddon.

But it did, as I've said, it did. In a sudden and special clarity, I realized why, because, oh, God, oh, God, if there were only the small horrors of the past—the bombing of an embassy, the crash of an airliner, the sinking of a ship, all small indeed if numbers were the only guide, not conscience, not morality, not any sense of humanity but cold numbers devoid of anything but mathematical precision and impersonality—then Satan's blood lust would have gone unquenched. For him, these "minor" atrocities were simply appetizers before the main feast.

I speak of that Final Battle described in the sacred pages of Scripture, that climactic clash at the end of history. For if God never truly fought back, then how weak He would seem, how empty His admonitions, how absurd those many proclamations of omnipotence and omniscience and all the rest in the face of what would be thus an inevitable victory for Lucifer, then-conqueror of Heaven, once-slum lord of Hell, the sum total of everything we had been through since leaving Heaven—only to win it all back.

How strange then, lost in such contemplation, there in the midst of that shattered terminal, cries piercing the air, people screaming for help, please, please help, how strange that the thought of my master having his way with the universe, the *opportunity* to recreate everything in *his* image, how melancholy it made me. I experienced not a fleeting moment of celebration, which I should have felt as one of his followers, as Milfult and DuRong and so on and so on and so on would undoubtedly feel, for they were more *into it*, as the expression goes, more attuned to the mission from the very start.

But for me, the journalist from Hell, not a single instant of pride was left, nothing of the kind but rather the terrifying sight of the aftermath of apocalypse. I had a vision of land after land piled high with his victims, from Rome to London to New York to Los Angeles, the Holy Ghost in chains of darkness forever, no longer a restraining influence, indeed only a defeated foe, the once transcendent might reduced to simpering impotence, mocked by creatures liberated from the dark alleys of their existence, and now parading before Him, venting their blasphemies. . . and next the Father and Son, my master reserving for his most profound enemies an unspeakable—

"Observer!"

That familiar intruding voice.

"Come! Do as your lord commands."

I looked at the dreaded one.

"Taste what I offer you from these diseased lips! Drink from the pool of death and decay!"

I did.

And it was good.

I *t is soon. The hard-line Soviets are poised. Reformer has only days of life left. . . .*

They are dressed as repair men, these Muslim filth, filth because of what they are, because of their very worship, because of what they are doing. They enter the basement of the hall, near the power generators.

"Allah will honor this," one of them whispers.

(Not Allah, fellow traveler. Nor Muhammed, that possessed charlatan.)

His comrade smiles, nods.

These two will do their work with a tiny fraction of the huge shipment of plastic-type explosives sent to a certain Middle Eastern country by a West German firm, enough to supply the needs of terrorism for more than a century, yet another indication that the scruples of German industrialists have not changed much since they cooperated with the Nazis for the slave labor from Auschwitz-Birkenau and other extermination camps.

Both men—are they to be called that, really? I know demons I like better than this sort of slime—have been close to the the region's most reprehensible despot, a maniacal beast more like my kind than any human being, a latter-day Hitler bent only on the satisfaction of his warped territorial desires and hunger for power.

Some time before, the world community found Saddam Hussein to be a monster, along with Muammar Muhamad a-Qadhafi, and such an opinion was correct, these scum unworthy of the leadership of any country. But the Middle East is prone toward the setting up of such individuals. One is almost guaranteed to emerge on the scene every few years. They all serve a bankrupt and satanic religion that will corrupt *any* who join it. And once my master has control, he will fling them out on some kind of battlefield, to do what he demands of them even as they carry the supposedly holy *Koran* by their side, and do their absurd, sometimes childish rites, claiming Allah's wrath on America and any other nation that gets in their way.

The two terrorists at the dome once were part of an elite Muslim guard until they disappeared from view two years earlier. It was assumed by the CIA that they had been executed for some infraction or other. But they had simply gone under-ground, to be trained for the Ultimate Mission, a code name for an act of such destructiveness that the leader they think they are serving now, known among us demons as Idiot-Muslim, will earn a place in the history books.

I look at Idiot-Muslim—this is only an arbitrary designa-tion, at least as applied to him because, as we know, all Muslims are idiots of the most pathetic sort, for how can they be described otherwise when they allow themselves to be chained to obeying a book as wretched as the *Koran*, a book whose pages are put to better use as toilet paper for human excrement than the source of any specious inspiration—yea, I look at Idiot-Muslim and I see a prototype of satanic perfection, a mindless automaton controlled in every respect by the Prince of Darkness. Even I, who sided with Satan from the start, would rejoice if someone cut out his throat and threw his body in the Sahara so that deserving buzzards could feast, and as many as possible from his heathen kind became additions to the carnage so that the world would be a bit less polluted, polluted as it is by their presence.

I am not surprised that Lucifer feels at home in the presence of Idiot-Muslim, for they are of a kindred bond. My master rejoices when a devil such as this one uses nerve gas to destroy his own countrymen because they dared to oppose him. It is said that he is not mad. It is said that he is quite a brilliant tactician. But, I ask, where did he obtain that brilliance, that complete and total amorality that is the foundation of everything he has done over the years?

I know the answer all too well.

*T*hat I am more enraged by such vipers than are millions of Christians is commentary richly evocative. It is not that Christians fail to become upset, of course; they do—and yet there is perhaps what might be called a "comfortable" edge to their anger. By and large they seem content to sit in their pews, and listen to their pastors, and return to their homes, and stuff themselves with food, and *tsk-tsk* at what is going on in the world.

Moral degenerates such as these—in Libya as well as Iraq and elsewhere—could slaughter an entire village, and decapitate every man, woman, and child, and *tsk-tsk* indeed the response would be. They could kidnap a diplomat, a clergyman, a school teacher, a crippled widow, they could kidnap anyone who catches their eye in the madness of the moment, and far too many Christians would shrug and shake their heads, and forget in a week or a month. When they are reminded, when they are confronted with the echo of that awfulness, they respond, oh, yes, they respond, *tsk-tsking* at the very mention of it, perhaps with a special collection or two for the bereaved families.

What drives countless numbers of Christians to greater uproar is not so much the moral aspects of those atrocities, or anything to do with the atrocities at all. If this kind of news were all that reached Western shores from the Middle East via the nightly television broadcasts, the newspapers, and the magazines, there would be concern, yes, and a few sermons might be preached about the barbaric Muslims, and then it all would die down.

But let *any* development in the Middle East affect their lifestyles, their wallets, and the decibel level goes up dramatically. A slaughter in Iraq or Kuwait is devastating, but let that slaughter be connected with *money*, let it affect the grocery bill or the gasoline bill or whatever in Oshkosh, Wisconsin, and *then* the hue and cry will become deafening.

These are the Christians who are comfortable in their faith, who find it reassuring, Christians who often do business with other Christians, who go to church with other Christians, play golf with them, and so on, and so on. It is a peaceful existence. Atrocities elsewhere in the world shake it but briefly, and then normalcy returns—but, ah, monetary influences rip it asunder, and repair is not so easy, not so quick.

If I were God, I would be weeping.

Other explosives are placed elsewhere. Like putting chewing gum under a theater seat.

Simple as that.

"Allah will bless us, Abdul," one of them says.

"Greatly," his companion agrees.

Allah will bless the maiming, the murder, the blinding, the deafening. Allah will rejoice over crushed skulls, caved in chests. He will stand in the middle of this new battlefield, and proclaim glorious victory!

In fact, that is what he does. He stands there, laughing harshly, this Allah of their worship.

A familiar sound to my kind.

We have heard it often.

*T*hose at the CMCI convention have less than an hour. It is midday. The noise of voices blending together is loud. Deals are being made. Deals everywhere. Free freight. Full return privileges. . . . I overhear Bookstore Manager talking with his wife, who co-owns Heavenly Choices Family Store. They are walking away from a booth where the publisher was eager to get their order.

"That was robbery," he tells her.

"I know," she agrees happily. "Great price."

"And sixty days billing!"

"Then add another sixty days for late payment."

"Four months to pay!"

"Won't they be reluctant to take our next order?"

"Publishers will do *anything* for a sale. Besides, we can dump them if necessary. There are *plenty* of others. Just *look* at them all!"

"It's true. We have to wait on the Lord for *our* money, you know."

They both break out laughing.

"It's a dog," the executive vice president chortles.

"I know, I *know*!" his assistant says, enjoying the moment as well.

"They thought they had us," the V.P. adds.

"Everybody knows they take forever to pay their bills," the assistant says. "Why would we give them anything good? They're too dumb to know the difference."

"We made them think that title was going to be a bestseller."

"Yet they were convinced they had *us* over a barrel."

Both men are licking their lips, and eagerly rubbing their hands together, as they await the next chance to witness for Jesus Christ, and to give Him the honor and the glory.

Big-Time Agent has his client, Name Author, at his side. They are having a meeting with the chairman of the board of Great Commission Books, one of the larger publishers, in a room in the basement of the great dome.

"His price doubles in six months if you don't renew the contract now," Big-Time Agent says softly, but with a steel core in his words.

"We just don't know," President replies. "Sales are good, but that *is* a great deal of money for a *ministry* to have to pay."

"Cut the crap," Big-Time Agent retorts.

"Crap?" President says, his eyes raised.

Big-Time Agent blushes.

"Sorry."

"You should be. This is God's business, you know."

"And I want to see God's author being treated as he should be. Are you going to agree or not? If I go out that door, you won't touch us again for less than a hundred twenty-five thou!"

Publisher leans forward.

"One hundred thousand, period."

Big-Time Agent starts to stand, as does Name Author.

"All right, all right," President says. "One hundred seven-teen five!"

Big-Time Agent smiles.

"It's a deal," he says.

They talk over a few more details, shake hands, then Big-Time Agent and Name Author leave.

President turns to an assistant.

"What crapola!" President exclaims.

"We get it back in royalties, as usual?" the assistant ventures.

"Absolutely! These guys bluster around a lot but they practically never ask for an audit."

"As a fail-safe, sir, should we play with the discount structure so that half-royalties kick in?"

"You're learning," President says. "You're learning real good."

Only half an hour now. Hidden clocks are ticking, ticking, ticking everywhere. . . .

Within minutes, Big-Time Agent and Name Author are with another publisher.

"We just negotiated a deal with Great Commission Books," he tells this CEO.

CEO is English, his mind bestirred with some reminders of the old days when publishing was still a gentleman's game.

"How much?" he asks simply.

"Hundred fifty thou," Big-Time Agent says without a flicker of his eyelids.

"That is quite a sum of money."

"My guy's worth it.

"He may be but—"

"If we walk out of here now, the price will be two hundred thou the next time. You save big bucks *this* time!"

CEO nodded.

"We'll talk," he says, thinking about that contractual clause dealing with a reserve held against returns.

At one end of the dome, near a side exit, an elderly woman is walking with her husband. They had had to sell their store after years of trying to make a go of it.

This is their last CMCI convention; they attended purely to be able to say goodbye to some old friends.

Hours had   passed. They are leaving now, tired, sad, casting one more glance back at the carnival, and whispering, "May God forgive them," just as they emerge out-of-doors, and the ground rumbles under their feet.

That couple is not alone. I see plenty of other men and women who, as they walk about the giant hall, shake their heads with embarrassment, and whisper among themselves about what is going on, the usurpation of the name of Christ for any commercial purpose.

May God forgive them, other servants of Christ echo those words about the bottomliners, the hucksters.

He will. If they ask.

But how many even *realize* the depths to which they are sinking? How many *understand* the blasphemy behind the merchandising of images and trinkets and the rest for profit? How many have rationalized themselves into a corner, and continue on as spiritually suicidal lemmings over a cliff, taking others with them, those who buy this stuff and put it in their homes, their offices, their cars as though they are paying homage to the Lord whereas they are only contributing to the cancer spreading throughout the land?

Oh, the carnival barkers of Christendom will protest if confronted, and issue forth with words about judgmentalism and the like, and they will flash sweet smiles of innocence, and then go on with their tacky spiels.

I remember Coney Island in the old days, you know. . . .

Where's the cotton candy, folks? The butter-dipped popcorn? The buy-a-kiss booth? (Everything else is for sale, why not that? Just say it's for a scholarship to send worthy kids to college, yeah, that usually guarantees some kind of support.)

Something else, come to think of it, I say to myself.
Where's the funhouse?

Suddenly I smile a demon-smile, a thin tongue darting out
from between my blood-red lips as I walk those aisles of greed.
You're in it, people. You're in it.

*I*t was not always the way it has become. Many years before, the mission of CMCI was quite simple: gather together the ministries and other organizations dedicated to the Great Commission through the use of all available media.

I remember attending the very first CMCI convention. Mifult accompanied me.

The speaker was Silver Hair.

"We have begun a mighty new thrust," he addressed the several hundred individuals in attendance at the small midwestern convention center. "There are exciting times ahead. But never let us forget the central purpose: the edification of believers, and the winning of new souls to Christ."

Mifult turned and looked at me, as I did with him.

"We have a tough battle ahead of us," he remarked. "They are very dedicated."

We saw examples of that dedication shortly thereafter. A publisher was exhibiting a book with a highly questionable theme. Silver Hair noticed it, and personally demanded that the publisher withdraw it. The publisher refused, and was then escorted from the hall, his booth closed down in the process.

That happened often over the intervening half-dozen years.

But then CMCI grew at an ever-increasing rate. More publishers opened up shop, more record companies, more ministries—all found the CMCI convention a magnet, the one arena in which they could individually and collectively offer themselves to the largest possible group of people.

T-shirts were introduced. Bumper stickers.

"The advent," Mifult would say later.

"Success for us," I told him sardonically.

The advent.

Indeed.

The advent of the junksters.

And also the beginning of the decline of CMCI.

"It is so much like its secular counterpart now," Mifult said a few years ago.

"Worse," I remarked. "With the others, there is no pretense."

Pretense. . . .

The plaything of satanic puppets seeking to justify what they do.

Today, in the midst of that sparkling new hall, I see a plain booth, a booth with a few tracts and some Bibles, and a dignified gentleman standing, looking at the passersby. Further down that particular row is a garishly-colored display on both sides of the aisle with scores of different books being offered. The publisher is greeting buyer after buyer, a broad smile on his face and a cash register for a brain—the smile quickly fades as soon as someone mentions the book he published a couple of years ago, supposedly the intimate revelations of a former bordello madam that was found out to be nothing but the sexual fantasies of a schizophrenic housewife in the Pacific Northwest, and he is suddenly called upon to apologize. While he is doing so, the buyer for an important chain of stores becomes irritated at being kept waiting, and starts to leave, and the publisher turns around and rushes after the buyer.

"Losing that fish would ruin his day," Mifult remarks.

"Indeed," I say.

At the end of the day, that dignified gentleman, smiling warmly, leaves the hall, grateful for the one individual who stopped at his booth, and to whom he could minister in faith, believing.

I re-enter the huge hall.
   I look at the bright colors.
   I listen to the din of collective voices.
   I stand for only a moment before the miseries are unleashed, engulfing those who are redeemed and dedicated to the saving of souls, together with those present only because there is money to be made, power to be gathered unto themselves and welded in defense not of the Kingdom of God but their own turf.

   I see a man, obviously quite old, sitting on a metal folding chair. He is looking around him.

   There are tears streaming down his blotched cheeks.

   I hear him whisper.

   I do hear him whisper.

   "Father, forgive them. . . ."

   He grows faint. His body tilts to one side.

   He sees me.

   "Are you—?" he asks in a raspy voice.

"No," I tell him, with a kind tone that is in opposition to my loathsome appearance.

I step aside then.

His concern evaporates. The tears are gone. There is now only joy.

"Are you the one to take me through the gates?" he asks as his soul takes leave of mortality.

The angel of light answers radiantly.

They go together past me, way, way past on a journey I can never take.

The old one's body slumps. This is noticed, but not immediately.

Some hot deals are being made, you know.

I can imagine hidden devices giving up their last few seconds.

Ticking-ticking-ticking. . . .

*T*he explosives go off.

That grand dome shakes like a giant beast, its concrete-and-steel-and-glass roar deafening. All communications with the outside world are instantly cut. No one can enter. No one can leave, all entrances and exits electrically controlled. The glass windows are unbreakable.

People are trapped.

The explosions have been timed. Periodically another set will go off. There is psychological warfare in this, apart from the very physical manifestations.

Idiot-Muslim knows all about madness, you see.

I walk among them. I have no host just now. Hosts can be cumbersome. Spirits have no limitations. I can flit from one end of the hall to the other.

I do.

I and others of my kind. Buzzing about. Prodding. Possessing. Doing what we do, at our master's command.

And we do very well. . . .

Arch Strutter is cowering in a corner, terrified. He is not thinking positively. He is not thinking at all, it seems. He is babbling nonsensical stuff while holding a paperweight that was to be his latest "gift" to those who supported his ministry; shaped like an abstract cross, it was covered by gold paint already turning green from the sweat of his palm.

A man running past sees Arch Strutter, spits at him, and rushes on.

But then I see the two young publishers who have rolled up their sleeves and are helping the seriously injured. The dark-haired one catches my attention—the front of his white shirt is stained red. Every so often he grimaces.

Demons pass *them* by.

But not Donald.

He is standing in the midst of what remains of the booth erected by his publisher. Earlier in the day there had been an announcement that a book by another author was withdrawn from publication because of a multitude of falsehoods in it, that particular author indulging a penchant for personal fantasy and dressing it up as non-fiction. The publisher is standing next to Donald, wondering why God has chosen to rebuke him so harshly, and all within such a short while. (That he would think God had destroyed an entire new building, affecting the futures of hundreds of firms, just to get back at *him* isn't reassuring about how he will come out of all this.)

Donald is rubbing his hands together, wishing that he had a Christian psychiatrist nearby, but not daring to admit it out loud.

The publisher, his five-hundred-dollar suit torn and dirty, is looking around at the devastation, and wondering if his firm can survive the shock of loosing a large chunk of the convention revenue that was to have been earned.

*W*reckage is everywhere.

People are crying. People are praying. People are dying by the dozen.

The man with the Scripture pencils is standing in the debris of his booth, thousands of them scattered all around him. He is holding a tattered sign boasting a 12 percent discount.

Silver Hair is cradling an old woman, her right arm hanging limply by her side.

"Grab hold of Jesus," he tells her.

She is crying.

"My chest!" she says so softly he can hardly hear her above the din. "I have a terrible pain in my—"

Silver Hair can do nothing but pat her giently and whisper Bible verses, but that is the best he knows, and he does it; he is not a doctor; there are no doctors around; there is only chaos,

He continues holding her lifeless body until someone tells him.

*R*obbie's mother never made it from that room. She regains consciousness. The tattered, bloody cloak that enfolded his soul is lying a few feet away. She crawls over to it, kisses his cheek one last time, wants to stay where she is, praying that she will join him in glory then and there. But people are crying, people are in pain, people need her as he did—and now that he is gone, that part of her yet remains. It cannot be ignored, buried under her grief, for she must continue honoring her Lord. She has little choice but to get to her feet, get to her feet, get to her feet, and help, if God will supply the strength.

He does.

*I*n the corridors outside the main hall there are more bodies, people who had been heading toward the exhibits or, having finished their business, were about to leave.

Now piled high.

Elderly ones. Children. The middle-aged.

The holocaust has entrapped them all.

I see banners.

"Save a whale—be a hero. Save a baby—be a jailbird."

I see Bibles clutched in death-frozen hands.

I see trinkets.

I see a terrorist stumbling toward me. He has just emerged from a doorway leading to the basement. He is mumbling something about Muhammed.

"I must be protected!" this craven one screams. "I must be protected from—from—"

In a split second I see the demon pursuing him.

No Name.

This one is so loathsome than no name can be found to describe him. He is worse in appearance, if that could be possible, than Satan. He has promulgated acts of atrocity that make many of the rest of us recoil.

And now No Name is on this man, this fool.

"Stand against the creature," I say mischievously, aware that No Name's greater malevolence makes my own seem less terrifying to him. "Proclaim Allah. Hold up Muhammed as your protector."

"Oh, yes, may my lack of faith be forgiven in this my moment of danger!"

He turns, faces No Name.

"I seek the protection of Allah," the terrorist says. "I seek the sheltering arms of Muhammed, the Lord's prophet and defender, *my* defender as well. You cannot stand against him!"

The demon roars with laughter.

"You do, huh?" he screams with sarcasm that erupts from him with festering disease from every sore.

The terrorist now stands proudly, with utter faith the spine of his defiance.

"I can sense the prophet reaching out toward me now."

"Good!" No Name says quietly now, his red-rimmed lips pressed closely together.

He reaches out those taloned hands toward the dying mortal in front of him.

"You see, blind one that you are, I *am* the prophet you claim, I am he whom you love. I, Muhammed, welcome you. . . . *for eternity!*"

The terrorist's heart abruptly stops beating. The breath of life passes from him, and that body of flesh and blood drops to the floor.

His spirit is seized by No Name's, and they stumble along the path to Hell together. . . .

How safe the architects of this infamy seem, at least those on the human side, of course, I tell myself, *planning as they did all this from their haven just outside Moscow, an estate far beyond the livelihood of 99 percent of the citizens over whom they hold sway. Such hypocrites—talking of the good of the motherland when what they are really trying to save are the tottering remains of the Communist Party—will gather soon around that same table as before, and they will be chuckling with delight. It has worked! It has worked! Soon their hired assassin will strike down Reformer. Soon—*

A trio has gotten together in the middle of the hall, trying to calm the hysterical masses with soft hymns. They have just finished *Nearer My God to Thee.* They are starting another: *"All hail the power of Jesus' name, Let angels prostrate fall. . . ."*

"Not that one!" Satan is screaming. "Stop them! Do something! I will never fall prostrate before anything but a statue of myself proclaiming my greatness."

Another explosion. More girders fall. More debris flies through the air. But that trio survives.

And they have started another hymn.

"Blessed assurance, Jesus is mine! O what a foretaste of glory divine!"

Satan stomps his cloven feet in front of them, shouting obscenities that they cannot hear, blasphemies only for the rest of us.

And there is a reason beyond simply the hymns.

Arch Strutter. . . one member of the trio.

"Are you washed in the blood, in the soul-cleansing blood of the Lamb?"

"DuRong!" Satan shrieks. "Come here *now!*"

DuRong obeys.

"I thought you would see to it that those words would *never* come from the lips of *that* man!" Satan demands.

"We lost him, master," my comrade replies simply.

"How?"

"A little child, looking for her mother in the wreckage, saw him, and came up to him, and said, 'Sir, my daddy is out of town and my mother is here but I can't find her. I can't find her. Would you help Jesus and me find her, please?'"

"And that was it? He caved in just like that?"

"He did, master. He did. He looked at her sweet face, her sweet, trusting face, and then at the cheap little trinket he had been holding. Then he got to his feet, threw that cross to one side, and walked with her, hand in hand!"

DuRong is acting strangely.

"Yes, yes, go on!" Satan blusters.

"I cannot tell you the rest."

"I order it."

DuRong hangs his head.

He does what the master expects of him.

"There is nothing. Childlike faith collapsed our years of deception. There is nothing more than that."

"Is she the one clinging to him now?" he sneers.

"Oh, yes. . . ."

Satan, disgusted, goes off to help in another part of the hall, not noticing DuRong's sardonic smile.

Arch Strutter and the little girl find her mother half-buried under debris.

He ministers to the two of them with great power and wisdom.

"Bless you," the woman says at the end of her life in the flesh. "Take care of my little girl."

"Mommy!" the little one cries.

The broken body is now lifeless.

"I want my Mommy back! Tell Jesus to bring her back!"

He is at a loss for what to say. Positivity wouldn't cut it. He cannot tell her the same old words. This is not the time, the place.

He bows his head momentarily.

A hand touches his shoulder.

He looks up.

The little girl is smiling through her tears.

"Jesus spoke to me," she tells him, her voice breaking. "He said He would take care of Mommy until we are together again."

Another explosion.

Part of the ceiling plummets.

Arch Strutter sees it. He pushes the little girl to one side. She escapes untouched. Arch Strutter does not. A chunk of concrete hits his temple. He falls inches from the child.

She runs over to him, plops down by his side, starts humming the only hymn she knows in its entirety, her mother's favorite: "*What a friend we have in Jesus, all our sins and griefs to bear. . . .*"

He closes his eyes.

"*Your little one will be fine,*" he tells the mother.

"*I know,*" she says as she takes his hand.

*T*he devastation draws fire departments from a hundred miles in every direction. FBI investigators are flown in directly from Washington, D. C. Local as well national news media descend on the scene. Frantic efforts are extended to save as many lives as possible, but one lingering problem is that the terrorists had planted *many* bombs to explode at various intervals—there is no way to know how many if any remain undetonated.

Firemen and other rescuers are added to the growing list of fatalities.

Finally—

"We can't send any more men in there for at least the next twenty-four hours," one of the fire chiefs tells an associate. "We've got to wait, to be sure that there won't be any more explosions."

"But some people must still be alive in there, sir," that associate reminds him.

"I know, I know, we've got a nightmare here. I pray to God that it's not too late for any of them."

It isn't.

The next day dozens are pulled from the wreckage.

And in the basement. . . .

I would never forget that group even as I stand in the lake of fire, surrounded by the punishment I so well deserve. Nothing could take them from my thoughts.

Ten human beings. Four elderly men and women, and six children under the age of ten, two just three years old.

They were in a small room that somehow had been left relatively untouched by the collapse of the dome. All around them were broken steel girders, and shattered glass, and great chunks of concrete—but that room was whole.

They were there because of a social program that provided for orphaned children to spend time with foster grandparents. None of the young ones had flesh-and-blood parents left. The CMCI executive board had flown them all in as a special ministry.

I stood to one side, watching little children sitting on the knees of old men and women, listening to prayers or hymns or other simple, kind words of attempted comfort, and little fear—what otherwise would have been massive waves of it largely swept aside as their faith took over, faith that was vibrant, that stayed firm and strong. Even as another blast shook what was left of the dome—and, yes, the children would cry a bit, would cling to their temporary guardians, depending on them for the kind of resolve that, in a large and frightening world, the little ones could not quite muster on their own—those elderly folks, accustomed to thinking about death, finding the moment joyful when they are able to dry tears other than their own, which took their own minds away from what had happened all around them.

K'Rupt came in as I stood there.

"Go after them," he said. "Destroy each and every one."

"No," I said.

"What was that?"

"No," I repeated.

"It is what Satan would want if he knew, if he were here as you and I are."

"No," I said a third time.

K'Rupt was livid, the rage coming out of every pore of him.

"Then I will do it myself!" he screamed.

"You can take their bodies, yes, but that is all you will be able to touch," I told him.

He looked at me.

"They all are redeemed?" he asked.

"Every single one."

He hurried to an old, old woman who was holding a three-year-old girl on her lap as the child slept with remarkable soundness. He was about to touch that wrinkled face, that ancient flesh when, suddenly, he was thrown back with such force that if he had been a physical being, and not one of spirit only, every bone in his body would have been smashed to powder.

Again and again he tried to enter the body of an old one or a child, and was tossed to one side.

"Damn them to hell!" he screamed.

"No, you are very wrong," I told him. "*They* are not the damned."

He had been stamping the floor with his twisted cloven feet.

. . . they are not the damned.

Those words struck him as though I had taken a fist and hit him squarely across the jaw.

He started weeping then.

"Oh, Observer, it is always thus with us," he said through the sobbing. "We cannot endure the cleansing that has purified their souls, and so we try to destroy them any way we can. We make the old bitter, and get them to commit suicide. We have the young born as drug addicts because of the sin of their mothers. And if we don't succeed with the old themselves, with the damnation of their souls, then we have our sport with their physical selves by motivating their so-called loved ones to fling them aside as forgotten human wrecks in some cold, hard institution where they no longer will be a bother."

A six-year-old boy was standing, singing a hymn, his eyes bright, his expression untroubled.

K'Rupt was only inches from him.

"If I could, Observer, I would rip him open right now and feast on his innards. But I cannot. So I will wait, and I will seek out an opportunity, later, instead to foster those circumstances that will rape his innocence and send him into the world on feet of revenge. Since he is redeemed, I cannot touch the soul of this child. But I can do a great deal to torment his mind, his emotions."

"Oh, yes, you can," I agreed, and added sardonically, "That is truly something to which you can look forward."

"But—" he started to say.

The hymn-singer finished. An elderly man with him had a sudden chest pain and fell back against the ground.

"Don't die," the little boy begged.

"You are safe," the man told him. "An army of angels is arriving to protect us."

"Are you sure?"

"Oh, yes, I see them now."

The old man was right.

For a moment Heaven had opened up, releasing a stream of angels directly into that room.

"They are so beautiful," he said, his voice fading fast.

He saw me then. He saw K'Rupt.

"How long have you been here?" he asked.

"For only a short while," I told him.

"You cannot harm any of them. You cannot touch a hair on the head of even this little one."

"Yes, I know."

He was gone, an angel taking him, and the two of them entering Heaven. In that instant, catching a glimpse, I saw the Son, the Blessed Son, and He saw me, and this divine one, this *Jesus Christus Theou Huios Soter* reached out to me, as He had done once before in the wilderness, and in that moment I could have broken away, one more chance to turn my back on the evil of many ages of time.

"*No!*" K'Rupt bellowed. "No, it cannot be."

"Oh, yes!" I shouted in anticipation. "Yes, it can. And if it can be me, it can be *both* of us, K'Rupt. *Now* we can leave the filth, the pain, the future we know to be ours otherwise. Now we can change all of that."

He hesitated, K'Rupt hesitated.

I stepped forward. An angel came to me, smiling.

"Welcome, Observer," this one called Blessed Assurance said.

K'Rupt was smiling.

"It is true, isn't it," he said.

"Yes indeed," another angel called Calvary's Mount replied with utter tenderness.

As the ascended Savior stood before the gates of Heaven, the two angels were ready to take us back with them. In an instant Heaven would be closed again.

A voice.

In the background, a voice.

Satan was calling.

"The master!" K'Rupt said. "We must not desert him. He needs us."

He pulled back.

"Break away," Calvary's Mount urged. "Just take my hand."

K'Rupt placed his talon in that angel-hand but as he did so, the talon was gone, and he had a hand like Calvary's Mount.

"Observer!" he said with astonishment. "Look!"

"Yes, I see," I told him. "Oh, God, loving, loving God, I *do!*"

My talon! Gone as well! We were doing it, praise God, yes!

And I could feel the accumulated miseries of long centuries being purged from my very being, a glow beyond description spreading—

That voice was stronger. Closer.

The master *wanted* us. The master demanded us.

And I had to admit something quite ghastly to myself, I had to admit that I enjoyed these massacres, that the satisfaction they stirred within me was pervasive, that I wanted to go and find others, and have their lives, their earthly, mortal lives torn from them, and watch the pain they endured as this happened.

It returned, that one vision of Armageddon, but it was not alone, a panorama of others, blood the uniting thread of all, blood everywhere, the blood of soldiers, of peasants, of assassinated presidents and murdered priests, graveyards all over the world filled with the residue of pleasurable acts.

. . . pleasurable acts.

It went beyond that one massacre, beyond garbage bags of babies, beyond the wasting away of AIDS patients as my kind and I tormented them unto death, and further on, all of this and deeper still, a pit so rancid, so—

I *wanted* it. I *wanted* every pint of blood. I *wanted* to wash my hands in the fluids that seep from crushed and torn bodies. I *wanted* anything that caused their screams to reach my ears so that I can thrill to—

No, I screamed. *No—! I have denied this before. It was only that one time, only with those missionaries. It could never be that way again. Never!*

But yes. But yes. But yes.

I heard Satan laughing in the background, laughing in ignoble victory over his duped slave, the master of deception finding me easy prey. As was K'Rupt, and all the rest of us.

K'Rupt pulled away from Calvary's Mount. I pulled away from Blessed Assurance.

In one ghastly surge, everything poured back in on us, my comrade and I, the filth just banished moments earlier now returned stronger than before, more damning than ever, because having known it all and then bid it goodbye, we had to succumb once again. And suffocated by that awful reality, we fled that room, leaving its aborted promise in our infernal wake.

*T*he flames in the giant hall have died down. I stand in front of the wreckage. Crosses lay on their sides, blackened. Scattered everywhere are signs of hoopla now fallen in mockery, banners proclaiming the triumph of Christian love alongside special quantity discounts.

We've won, I think with sorrow. *We've crushed—*

No!

I won't let myself succumb to such deception, though I belong to the deceivers, if unwillingly, if wishing it could be different while knowing it never will.

Not crushed! my mind shouts. *It only seems that way. You look merely at the residue of one battle, foolishly presuming it to signal the direction of the war.*

Lucifer stands next to me.

"Wonderful sight," he says. "All their hypocrisies lying in waste!"

He is trembling with delight.

"The media will be our greatest servants," he adds. "They will spread the news throughout the civilized world."

Lucifer knows the routine well. He had used the media often in his pursuit of domination—newspapers, magazines, books, television, and radio becoming puppet outlets for seductive heresies and whatever else he cared to disseminate.

"I can imagine what those news shows will do with this!" he adds. "Perhaps it will consume their entire broadcast time. They are never less than hungry for anything that will promote their hidden agenda. And I know better than anyone that they *do* have one! Something wonderful to anticipate, don't you agree, Observer?"

I nod like the robot I have become, programmed to obey, and only that.

"Write it all in your book," he tells me, his hideous frame spewing forth the filth and disease of centuries, geysers of yellow-green fluids from continually bursting sores. "Those glorious moments must be immortalized."

He moves with effort, a weariness belying the aura of triumph he is trying so hard to project.

"I want every detail described perfectly," he rambles on, his lips curled into a curious smile that I have not seen before, and I am tempted to ask him what has amused him at that very moment. But I do not, remaining silent in my puzzlement. "Some of those ministries will never recover, especially the ones built on the vision of a single man. Take away the man, and there is no other foundation, so it becomes like dust."

He turns to me, puts one hand on my shoulder.

"Miss nothing, Observer. That is your assignment, and so it has always been. Capture it all, for you have never had any other purpose. Remember, I trust you to write the truth, Observer."

I smile though he knows not why.

. . . I trust you to write the truth.

How easily those words come, Lucifer, master, devil! How you brandish about that which you have tried to corrode in humankind, and now you expect *us* to be worthy somehow.

My book, precious journal, eons of thought and deed, this is all that will be left in my wake at the end.

A Book of the Days of Observer, Once an Angel of Light.

"I hear what you say," I assure the devil.

"Good! Good! As your reward, I will see that it is required reading past the Gates of Heaven."

"As it is in Hell?" I ask, shivering though unnoticed.

"How right you are," he replies. "How right you are."

Satan laughs then, loudly, coarsely, as is his way—but this time for a reason unknown.

I think of my book of the ages, its chapters of blood and sin and—

Yea, I do as my master asks, as I have always done.

I capture the moments. I capture the moments.

Every last one.

There was an instant, after Darien had been rescued from Hell by ever-present Stedfast, that my master's resolve cracked and bent, though he snapped back in defiance quickly enough.

He had tried hard to seduce the purity that Darien represented, rebellious purity perhaps, but purity nevertheless. Satan used every weapon, every trick, every sinful overture at his disposal.

None worked in the end.

I remember Darien begging me to break away from Satan. I wavered, as always, and as I have said before, and often in this journal of mine, I could have joined him, could have been also pulled from that sulfurous place—but as the master approached, as he called to me yet again, yet again, yet again, any flash of courage, any residue of willpower dissolved and I went to Satan, managing nothing more than a whimper of shame.

Gone.

Darien was gone then, Stedfast's intercession quite sufficient to take him from ten thousand upon ten thousand monstrosities hovering, and I one.

I could see Stedfast looking at me, not in hatred nor shame but love, love sublime, love that did not pity, love that was unimpeded because it was only itself, nothing to dilute it in any way, love flowing out to touch me, and I knew that it was his own, indeed it was, but mixed with love from Someone else. I said goodbye to Stedfast, I said it in my mind and my heart, and he turned away, and that was it, no more moments ever again like that one.

Satan had walked ahead of the rest of us, and stood there, looking upward, looking upward as, for an instant, we all shared the same recollection of that place to which Darien and Stedfast ultimately would be traveling, that blessed place, the one we gave up, the one—

Through the volcanic-like geysers, there was for an instant, barely visible, the bent-over shape of a wretched creature falling to his knees, weeping.

And in the background, we hear, faintly at first, then the sounds coming ever louder, the early hints of portended battle starting on war's prophetic field.

*R*eformer dead . . . hours after he pledged support for the Americans against the nation responsible! That faithful aide is wounded, too, but not fatally; he quickly hides a small leather-bound book that the general secretary had been carrying at that precise moment, hides the volume because no one else would understand the *why* of it.

The world is stunned at these atrocities.

In the United States, millions rise up in anger and demand swift revenge, revenge for those who had been murdered, and for Reformer as well.

The President is asked to retaliate. He wavers. With Reformer's support, there was a chance that the two countries could act together, that they could stun the critics into silence by this very cooperation.

But someone new is in charge of the U.S.S.R.

A leader from the old guard. Everyone else thought the old guard was dead, crumbling like the walls that once secluded it from the world.

But things are different now.

Very.

And from somewhere in the Middle East, a man rises up, talking peace. . . .

Epilogue

I LOOK ABOUT ME. I SEE DEMONKIND AND HUMAN-kind together, writhing in agony, as I have been doing.

I see Hitler.

I see mass killers Manson . . . Gacy.

But not Bundy, no, not Bundy.

I see a preacher who claimed in his mortality to have been the Lord's instrument for life immortal, just send in the green-backs to keep him going.

I see that actress, the one whose exercise routines mean little now.

I see many presidents, many senators, many mayors and governors and police chiefs, side-by-side with drug dealers and x-rated movie producers, and countless others.

I see nuns and rabbis. I see Muslims, Buddhists, Mormons, others. I see Baptists, Presbyterians, Pentecostals, Lutherans, Episcopalians, Seventh Day Adventists, Nazarenes, Quakers—each and every denomination, group, sect represented here in the midst of damnation.

They never realized that the label itself, the form, the ceremony were not enough.

I see millionaires. The very poor. White. Black. Yellow. Sane. Mad.

The lake of fire gives no place to bigotry, to status.

I see painters, poets, so-called Christian rock singers.

Some of you were right on, and went the way of the redeemed. But some of you ended up here, the flames searing your pretense.

I see those gay, those straight.

I see the radiant Son of God!

He is walking among us. Souls are reaching out for Him but He must tell one what He must tell all: "It is too late, my lost sheep."

He stops before me.

His gaze reaches into the very center of my being.

Something is in His hands, hands free of Calvary's scars.

"These are some of the bits and pieces of your book, Observer."

I see his arms holding a large pile of scrolls, of diaries, of random sheets of paper that somehow do not burn up right away, that do not burn because they are protected as long as they are in His arms, as long as they are sheltered by Him.

"Look at them, Observer," Lord Jesus the Christ says.

I obey the Son, I obey Him at least this once, this final time. I can scarcely believe what I see or, rather, do not see, as He hands me scroll after scroll, sheet after sheet, each burning to ashes even as my eyes scan them, even as my eyes see the monstruous, the oppressive, the maddening truth.

I look into that face again, those eyes, hear that voice telling me what my mind cannot wholly grasp in that moment.

"Your hosts, Observer . . . they were just another excuse wrapped in the dementia of your kind," He says with no satisfaction. "You were not as committed to Satan's cause, so he used this book. It was a trick, Observer, a trick to get you to lead them into damnation."

All that time! Centuries piled high upon one another. Entering host after host.

And for no reason except to camouflage the damned truth about my weak and pitiable self.

He drops the other pages at His feet. They are gone in an instant, they are gone as is the whole reason for being to which I had clung, with which I was deluded for so very long.

"Lord Jesus?" I ask, sobbing.

He hesitates, turns, waits for the question that He knows already.

"A *real* entry, please?" I beg. "No more lies. . . ."

He nods.

"Have you no pitiable scrap upon which I can write?" I ask, trembling.

I reach out the talon that is my hand, in anticipation, thinking that He will do this for me, thinking that there is something I have to say that can survive the thirsty flames.

He seems quite sad, and I imagine—or is it real?—a single tear rolling down one cheek.

"It is no use, is that not so, *Jesus Christus?*" I say with certainty that astonishes me.

His very manner seems answer enough.

. . . the truth.

Oh, dearest Lord! Can it be so, that when You pass by, as You must, on your way to the new Heaven, the new Earth, can it be so that I *am* to remain behind?

Yes, it can, Observer, it surely can, it surely is, He says, though only with His expression, the whole of His countenance, words unnecessary just now.

Now the Son of God leaves the flames. Now the saints await.

There has been spread out before me, and perhaps for all of eternity, a revelation as tormenting, it may seem later, as the flames themselves, it and they as one.

My hosts. . . .

Needless players in a farce.

I wanted only their anguish, feasting upon every inevitable moment of it, cloaked as it was in my dreary conceit, that pathetic and doomed scenario of self-justification that had kept me going, kept me going, kept me—

A Book of the Days of Observer, Once an Angel of Light.

Never would it be compiled from fragments written across the centuries, a kind of Satanic bible demanded by my master.

A Book of the Days of Observer—

The flames were not to blame, you know. They could not consume what never was, what never could be.

Mine.

And mine alone.

Wrenched from the possessed and accumulated miseries of unwary human slaves as they went through the pointless motions of my deceit.

I turn to Satan, I turn to Lucifer the Magnificent, and see his expression, see the lingering shards of his cruel hoax written on that awful face, see that he knew, that he had known from the beginning, that this was just his way of getting me to—

I might as well not have existed, for even an instant. What was the reason of it, what was the purpose, what was there to drive me on in continued rebellion against the only One who could have given me hope, real hope, not the doomed ravings to which I succumbed. . . ?

I look around me again, from Satan to Mifult to Muhammad, who was supposedly so good, so noble, yet in reality nothing more than another deluded figure manipulated by my master—all caught up in the destiny wrought by what they became—and the millions, the countless doomed they dragged into the flames along with them.

A Book of the Days—

My book . . . my book.

So easily reduced to nothingness.

Every last blank page.

Oh, my Lord, my Lord!

There is then from one end of that lake of unalterable judgment to the other the awful echoes of shrieking madness torn from these my phantom lips forever and ever . . . *and ever.*

A Bo.k of the Da.s of Obs..ver, Once an Ang—

It was to have been the master volume, the one into which all the scraps from centuries past were to be compiled, now gone in dust, trod underfoot by lions and lambs and bright-faced redeemed led by joyous cherubim travelling Angelwalk toward a golden temple rising out of the mists atop a majestic mount called Sinai.

Somewhere in the air perhaps are cries of pain, cries from ten thousand upon ten thousand throats, and a single sad and soon lost voice, "It is gone, it is gone and none, none at all have ever, ever read it, because there is nothing in its pages, and there never has been."

Finally, in all the ways that matter, truly, truly matter, through time and space and eternity, Observer is no more.

And no one knows. No one knows.

The deeds we do, the words we say,
Into still air they seem to fleet,
We count them ever past;
But they shall last—
In the dread judgment they
And we shall meet.
John Keble

Finis